Perfect Punctuation

Stephen Curtis was an English lecturer for ten years and since 1988 has worked as a freelance lexicographer, translator and writer. He contributed to *The Encarta World English Dictionary* and *The New Penguin English Dictionary* and wrote, with Martin Manser, *The Penguin Writer's Manual* and *The Facts on File Guide to Style*.

Other titles in the *Perfect* series

Perfect
Punctuation

Stephen Curtis

BOOKS

Published by Random House Books 2007

2 4 6 8 10 9 7 5 3 1

First published in the United Kingdom in 2007 by
Random House Books

Random House Books
Random House, 20 Vauxhall Bridge Road,
London SW1V 2SA

www.randomhouse.co.uk

Addresses for companies within The Random House Group Limited
can be found at: www.randomhouse.co.uk/offices.htm

The Random House Group Limited Reg. No. 954009

A CIP catalogue record for this book
is available from the British Library

ISBN 9781905211685

The Random House Group Limited makes every effort to ensure that the
papers used in its books are made from trees that have been legally sourced
from well-managed and credibly certified forests. Our paper procurement
policy can be found at: www.randomhouse.co.uk/paper.htm

Typeset in Minion by Palimpsest Book Production Limited,
Grangemouth, Stirlingshire
Printed in the UK by CPI Bookmarque,
Croydon CR0 4TD

Contents

Introduction

To the reader

I should very much like to begin this book by assuring my readers that mastering the art of punctuation is not only vital for their success and happiness in life, but also tremendous fun.

Honesty, unfortunately, will not allow me to make either of these claims. Punctuation is a relatively modest art and a servant to other aspects of writing. You are never likely to read a book review that says, 'The plot is predictable, the characters are boring and the style is lifeless, but all this is redeemed by some magnificent punctuation.' On the other hand, if the plot, characters and style are magnificent, but the author's punctuation leaves something to be desired, you are unlikely to be put off from reading the book. You can get by without knowing the finer points of punctuation, just as you can get by without knowing how to spell difficult words, where to find China on a map of the world, when the Battle of Hastings took place, or what is meant by H_2O. Certain, perhaps rather peculiar, people may wince, or foam at the mouth, when they read a label saying 'POTATO'S' in a greengrocer's shop, but they do not mistake the potatoes for tomatoes or oranges on that account – or necessarily refuse to buy them – do they?

You can get by, usually, because other people will fill in the gaps in your knowledge or skill for you. Also, the human mind is programmed to try to make sense of things. A hastily scrawled note

OF TILL 2 TAKE CALLS 4 ME TA ☺

or a text message is not altogether incomprehensible because it takes liberties with grammar, spelling and punctuation and mixes words, numbers and symbols. Readers, often in a hurry themselves, want to understand. Consequently, and out of the goodness of their hearts, they will do the necessary interpretive work for the writer.

The fact that you have bought this book, or simply picked it up to look at it, perhaps means that you do not want simply to get by or be, like Tennessee Williams' heroine in *A Streetcar Named Desire*, 'always . . . dependent on the kindness of strangers'. Correct punctuation and spelling may be fairly modest accomplishments, but if you can punctuate and spell, you can at least be a net contributor to understanding and clarity and not an intellectual scrounger. You will also run less risk, if this is important to you, of being considered 'ignorant', 'uneducated' or a person who is, however inadvertently, contributing to the decline of the English language or, indeed, civilisation as we know it.

The purpose of this book

The final sentence of the previous paragraph introduces a rather delicate topic. The purpose of this book, as the title suggests, is to perfect your punctuation – or, if that seems too ambitious an aim, to try to explain the purpose and function of the various punctuation marks and enable you to use them with confidence. However, this is not a campaigning book. What you do with any knowledge or skill you gain from it is your own affair, but it is not primarily intended to put you in a position to pour scorn on people who misuse apostrophes or semicolons. There is a lot of fun to be had from spotting howlers of all sorts. There is more fun in mispunctuation, misspelling and misuse of language, probably, than in correct punctuation, spelling and style. But there is, or there ought to be, pleasure in doing anything well, whether it is making something, writing something or even punctuating something. If this book enables you to experience some of that kind of pleasure, it will more than have fulfilled its aim.

Language and writing style are always changing. This change is a fairly gradual process, but it is a continuous one. Writers used punctuation differently fifty or a hundred years ago. People who wrote about punctuation then would likewise have offered different advice or instructions to their readers. (It may come as a relief to the reader to know that nowadays punctuation is less complex than it used to be, and that there is, generally speaking, less of it.) In another fifty or a hundred years' time, things will, no doubt, have changed again. Obviously, this book can only provide information about the current situation; a more important point to note, however, is that correctness can only be assessed on the basis of what is correct now and, more often than not, what is considered correct now is based on what was considered correct in the past.

It may often seem that people who care about language are simply trying to hold a door shut either against a tide of new ideas and practices or against a horde of ignorant and uneducated vandals whose aim is to destroy the English that they love. If this is what they are trying to do, it is bound in the end to be a vain endeavour. *Hopefully*, in the sense of 'it is to be hoped that', still causes controversy, at least among purists, even though the word, according to *The New Oxford Dictionary of English*, is used far more frequently now in this new sense than in the old (*The dog saw me putting on my shoes and stood up hopefully*), which surely proves that many if not most people find the new sense useful. There is no language police to arrest a word that breaks through the door. Dictionaries, and the other works that we go to for authoritative advice on language, eventually swim with the tide. Most dictionaries, in fact, trumpet the number of new words they contain, which are, in some cases, words that purists might originally have shuddered at. If enough users of English decided that 'potato's' was a correct way to spell the plural of *potato*, that usage would eventually creep into the dictionary and into books such as this one. We are still a long way from that, however.

We need perhaps to think about correctness in a different way, not so much as an exercise in shutting things or people out or rescuing a beloved language from barbarians, but as something that we get a modest pleasure from because it is a good thing in itself. It is good to be educated and to be able to speak and write clearly and correctly according to the standards of the time in which we live. It may not be cool, it may not be sexy, but it is a good thing and it is a useful thing. Unless we believe that somewhere deep down, the 'barbarians' have already won and taken over.

Using language well is one way of putting this belief into practice. I am, I hope, not alone in arguing that you cannot use language really well, unless you can punctuate at least adequately. That is my reason for writing this book. I hope it is your reason for reading it.

The purpose of punctuation

The basic purpose of punctuation is to organise words in a way that helps the reader understand precisely what the writer meant to say. Punctuation, as I said earlier, is a servant to other aspects of writing. Words do most of the work – a writer has to be able to choose the right words to express his or her ideas – but badly organised words obscure meaning. Punctuation should clarify it.

To illustrate the point that punctuation can affect meaning, let me use a very simple example. The words *drop dead gorgeous* can be punctuated in at least two different ways. Punctuated like this:

> *drop-dead gorgeous*

they mean one thing; punctuated like this:

> *Drop dead, gorgeous!*

they mean something else entirely.

For a slightly more subtle example, consider this sentence from an earlier paragraph:

> *Unless we believe that somewhere deep down, the 'barbarians' have already won and taken over.*

If we move the comma in that sentence, the meaning changes:

> *Unless we believe that, somewhere deep down the 'barbarians' have already won and taken over.*

Punctuation affects meaning. We might put it more strongly: punctuation creates meaning. If that sounds like a bit of an over-statement, it is certainly true that bad punctuation can destroy meaning at least as effectively as bad spelling:

> *I asked him politely, as I thought why he was making such a racket, at this time of night?*

If the sentence is punctuated correctly, the meaning is restored:

> *I asked him, politely as I thought, why he was making such a racket at this time of night.*

There are rules that tell you where to put commas and when to use question marks, and these rules are given in the relevant chapters of this book. Good punctuation, however, is not simply a matter of rules. It also has a lot to do with common sense and with your basic feeling for language.

In one of its more old-fashioned senses, the noun *stop* means a punctuation mark. Most punctuation marks represent a brief 'stop' or 'pause' in the flow of a sentence. When we are speaking, we use various methods to help put our meaning across, such as raising our voice slightly at the end of a question. We also naturally tend to insert fractional pauses between certain groups of words:

> *Listen carefully meet me outside the town hall at six*
> *o'clock oh and don't forget to bring the you know what*

You should not write this like that, but, more to the point, you would never say it like that. You would normally say:

> *Listen carefully meet me outside the town hall at*
> *six o'clock oh and don't forget to bring the*
> *youknowwhat*

What you would normally say gives you at least a rough guide as to how to punctuate:

> *Listen carefully. Meet me outside the town hall at six*
> *o'clock – oh, and don't forget to bring the you-know-*
> *what.*

It is usually a good idea to say things over to yourself, either aloud or with your 'inner voice', as you write them or after you have written them, in order to check that they 'sound right', that is, natural and clear. The same practice will help you get your punctuation right. Certainly, if you read sentences like this previous example aloud, pausing at the commas:

> *I asked him politely, as I thought why he was making such a racket, at this time of night?*

you are unlikely to let them pass.

A final word about this book

It is difficult to talk or write about any aspect of language use without using a certain number of technical terms and referring occasionally to grammar. I have tried throughout this book to explain things as straightforwardly as I can, only resorting to grammatical rules and terminology where there is no real alternative. It is, however, particularly hard to understand punctuation, which mainly organises words into and within sentences, if you are unaware of how sentences work. The very first chapter of this book, therefore, is devoted to the sentence and goes into a certain amount of grammatical detail. Readers who are confident that they understand sentences and such matters as the difference between a main clause and a subordinate clause are cordially invited to skip this chapter and continue with those devoted to individual punctuation marks.

1 Sentences and final punctuation marks

The sentence

It may seem slightly perverse to begin a book about punctuation by talking about 'the sentence'. If, however, I started with the grand announcement that all sentences begin with a capital letter and most end with a full stop, you would probably tell me to pass on rapidly to something a bit more challenging. The question of what a sentence is, or of whether or not a particular set of words makes up a proper sentence, perhaps falls into that category. This question is also very relevant to the use of punctuation. If you do not know when a string of words achieves the status of a proper sentence, how do you know where to put a full stop, question mark or exclamation mark? Moreover, a general discussion of the sentence is relevant not only to these particular marks, which will be dealt with in this part of the book, but also has a bearing on others such as the colon and semicolon, to which we shall be turning later.

The basics

The New Oxford Dictionary of English defines a sentence as:

> a set of words that is complete in itself, typically containing a subject and a predicate, conveying a statement, question,

exclamation, or command, and consisting of a main clause and sometimes one or more subordinate clauses.

This definition is admirably straightforward for someone who has a basic knowledge of the vocabulary used in discussing language and grammar. Nevertheless, someone who is unfamiliar with that kind of vocabulary may still have a problem using that definition, clear and accurate though it is, to decide whether the following are sentences or not:

Why

Go

The fat cat sat

When all is said and done

If you can keep your head when all about you are losing theirs and blaming it on you

(Punctuation marks have been omitted here because their presence, assuming they were used correctly, would give the game away – which is, indirectly, a sure sign of how necessary they are in ordinary writing.)

The answer is that the first three examples are complete sentences, while the last two are not.

It is possible that at the same time as you were taught that a sentence begins with a capital letter and ends with a full stop, you were also taught that a sentence must contain a verb (a word such as *go*, *come*, *think*, *disturb*, *disestablish* or *discombobulate* that describes an action) and a subject (generally a word such as *cat, car, woman, plumber, sentence* or *sententiousness*, describing a thing, person, animal, quality or state and called a noun). The subject carries out or is affected by the action referred to by the verb. While this is generally or typically true, it is not true in all cases. The crucial part of the dictionary definition given above is the phrase 'a set of words that is complete in itself'. That is what makes it possible for a single word such as *why*, at least in the form of a question, to function as a sentence:

> 'I've decided to sell everything I own and give the proceeds to charity.' — 'Why?'
>
> 'The car's broken down again.' — 'Blast!'
>
> 'Can I come with you?' — 'Yes.'

The three single words that form the responses in each of these fragments of dialogue all count as good and proper sentences (although, strictly speaking, they should be called 'minor sentences' to distinguish them from the standard type). They are complete in themselves: no more needs to be said to communicate the idea that the speaker has in mind. Perhaps the best words to latch onto if you have any difficulty with the idea of 'completeness in itself' are *yes* and *no*. In many, many contexts they say it all; everything else is simply embroidery.

It may be a little difficult to grasp the notion that a single word that is not a verb can form a complete sentence. It may be even more difficult to understand why a much longer set of words, which contains a subject and a predicate (the part of a sentence that contains a verb and says something about the subject), does not count as a proper sentence. Let us call up one of the previous examples again.

> *When all is said and done* . . .

Imagine someone saying this to you and stopping after *done*. Your first instinct surely would be to produce a complete sentence in reply: 'What?' When all is said and done, what? In common-sense terms, something remains to be communicated. We know from everyday experience that people use this phrase as a prelude to something else:

> *When all is said and done, he's still only a child.*
>
> *When all is said and done, she's been an excellent mother to those children.*

But we perhaps need to back up common sense with a little grammar. It is the word *when* that prevents the phrase from being a proper sentence. Although it sounds rather awkward and high-flown, *All is said and done* is a proper sentence. *When* and words like it such as *where, whether, how, (al)though, as, because, unless, since* and *if* act as what are known as subordinating conjunctions when they appear at the beginning of statements. Some of them can introduce questions that form complete sentences:

> *Where are you?*
>
> *How did she do that?*

But when a word of this type comes at the beginning not of a question, but of a statement, it makes that statement incomplete:

> *Where you are . . .*
>
> *How she did it . . .*

Common sense tells us that anyone who says something like this and then stops is guilty of withholding information. These phrases cry out to be part of something larger:

> *Where you are is where I want to be.*
>
> *I expect the weather is glorious where you are.*
>
> *How she did it remains a mystery.*
>
> *If I knew how she did it, I'd do it too.*

Subordinating conjunctions begin statements that form parts of sentences, but that need something else added to them to become full sentences. They are useful indicators that a string of words that looks like a sentence may not, in fact, be one:

> *If you can keep your head when all about you are losing theirs and blaming it on you . . .*

When you use one, check carefully to make sure that it forms part of something that is complete in itself before you insert a full stop.

The main clause

In grammatical terms, subordinating conjunctions begin subordinate clauses, and, grammatically, a standard sentence cannot consist of one subordinate clause or a number of subordinate clauses alone: it must have a main clause.

What, then, is a clause and how do you distinguish a main clause from a subordinate one?

A clause is a set of words that contains a subject and a predicate; a main clause is a clause that is not introduced by a subordinating conjunction and contains a finite verb.

I said nothing.

is a main clause

Although I said nothing . . .

is a subordinate clause.

If the definition of a clause looks similar to the definition of the sentence given at the beginning of this section that is only right and proper, for a sentence can consist of a single clause, so long as that clause is a main one.

Let us go back to the only one of our original five sentences that is a proper sentence of the ordinary kind:

The fat cat sat.

This has a subject *cat* and a finite verb *sat*. It has one clause: a main clause. We can add any amount of material to this clause, before it, after it or inside it, and so long as it remains intact, we can call what we have created a proper sentence:

The fat cat sat where the thin dog had been sitting a few moments before.

Having finished his milk and licked his whiskers, the fat cat sat.

The fat cat, never the most energetic of animals, sat.

A new concept has suddenly appeared in the discussion: a 'finite verb'. It is easier to say what a finite verb is not than what it is.

It is not, first of all, a verb preceded by *to*, as in *to be, to do, to think*, etc. That form is known grammatically as an 'infinitive', it is 'infinite' insofar as it refers to the action as such, divorced from any particular person or thing carrying it out. Being 'infinite', it cannot logically be finite, so

> *To be frank*

and

> *To hope for the best*

cannot be main clauses.

Neither does a present participle or *-ing* form of verb count as a finite verb when it stands alone. Consequently,

> *Weather permitting*

cannot be a main clause, and

> *All other things being equal*

and

> *Judging by what she told me last week*

cannot be main clauses either.

Nor does a past participle (a form of the verb that usually ends in *-ed*) count as a finite verb when it stands alone, which rules out

All things considered

as well as

Point taken

and

Gone fishing

as main clauses too.

Finally, a main clause is not a combination of both these types of participle.

Having settled my affairs and put everything in order

is not a clause containing a finite verb and cannot function as a main clause.

On the positive side, most of the verb forms that we use every day are finite ones, including two-part verbs containing present or past participles or infinitives.

In the following examples, the finite verbs are shown in **bold** type:

*Picking up his hat and coat, Henry **followed** me out.*

*To dare **is** to do.*

*Once assembled, the machine **is subjected** to a variety of tests.*

*To be perfectly honest, I **don't know**.*

*You **will take** me with you, **won't you?***

*I **think** I **am going** to be sick.*

*He **had indicated** some time before that this **is** what he **might do.***

The basic rule that a sentence should be 'a set of words that is complete in itself' would rule out many of the examples containing non-finite verbs, shown above. However, that same rule would qualify several of them to be minor sentences and end with a full stop:

'Can we go out tomorrow?' — *'Weather permitting.'*

Equipped with all this information, we should now be able to identify a main clause. It should, you may remember, contain a subject and a predicate, and the predicate should contain a finite verb. The main clauses in the following examples are also in bold type.

*When he got home after the party, **he went straight to bed.***

*Not knowing what to do next, **she asked her best friend for advice.***

*Undeterred by the bad publicity, **they went ahead with the product launch.***

***We'll sort all that out** when they actually get here.*

That, when all is said and done, is what really matters.

Go now, before it starts to rain again.

The main clause in the final example sentence appears not to have a subject, but when the verb is in the imperative (the form used to give a command), a subject is implied even though it is not stated. It consists of the person or people who are being commanded to do something:

(You must) Stop it, before someone gets hurt.

There is a great deal more that could be said about sentences. It is possible, for example, for a sentence to have two or more main clauses, which are connected by linking words such as *and*, *or* or *but*, or by a semicolon:

I like curry, and the hotter the curry the better I like it.

She went one way; I went the other.

But we are not principally concerned here with sentence construction, rather with finding out what makes a proper sentence so that we know where to put a full stop. It is time to pay more attention to punctuation specifically. Before we do, however, there is time for one final aside.

The first two lines of Kipling's most famous poem *If –* have been given more than once as an example in the previous paragraphs. One of the poem's many remarkable features is that all its thirty-two lines constitute one single sentence; the main clause is not reached until the last line but one (and then Kipling provides two main clauses). I will quote the closing lines here, in proper form, and leave you to pick out the main clauses:

> *If you can fill the unforgiving minute*
> *With sixty seconds' worth of distance run,*
> *Yours is the Earth and everything that's in it,*
> *And – which is more – you'll be a Man, my son!*

Recap

- A sentence is a set of words that is complete in itself, that is, that can be understood as saying all that is necessary to convey an idea or a response to a question.

- A sentence can be a statement, question or command and ends with a full stop, question mark or exclamation mark.

- A clause is a set of words that contains a subject and a predicate.

- A main clause must have a finite verb in its predicate.

- A main clause that is a statement does not open with a subordinating conjunction.

- A standard sentence must contain a main clause and may consist simply of that main clause.

Exercise

Find the finite verbs in the following sentences:

1) *You are wanted urgently back at the office.*

2) *Encouraged by their early success, they decided to expand their operations.*

3) *Buying lottery tickets is like throwing money down the drain.*

4) *We shall be going whatever the weather.*

Find the main clauses in the following sentences:

5) *Whether we like it or not, we have to follow their instructions.*

6) *Fortifying himself with a sherry, he sat down to read the report.*

7) *Skip the first paragraph because I'm going to cut it.*

8) *When you've finished using the sewing machine, would you mind putting it away?*

The Full Stop (.)

The basics

The full stop is used to close any sentence that is not a question or an exclamation. Because the full stop marks the end of the sentence, as a general rule no sentence should contain more than one full stop. This applies particularly in cases where you are quoting what someone else has said or written and what that person said or wrote constituted a complete sentence. The only exception to the one-full-stop-per-sentence rule is when a full stop has been used in an abbreviation.

Closing a sentence

The previous section has provided plenty of examples of the main use of the full stop and has already dealt with the issue of when a set of words constitutes a full sentence and so requires a full stop (or question or exclamation mark) at its end.

It is usually easy enough to distinguish between sentences that are statements, and so require full stops, and sentences that are questions or exclamations:

> *Your time is up.*
>
> *Is the time up yet?*
>
> *Time's up!*

The important thing to remember is not to put a full stop after something that is not a complete sentence.

NOT
I'm going. Whether they give me permission or not.

but
I'm going, whether they give me permission or not.

NOT
Covered from head to foot in mud. She was virtually unrecognisable.

but
Covered from head to foot in mud, she was virtually unrecognisable.

NOT
He asked me a very silly question. To which I did not bother to reply.

but
He asked me a very silly question, to which I did not bother to reply.

It is also standard practice to place the full stop immediately after the last letter of the last word of the sentence, leaving no gap. The only thing that should ever come between the final letter of the final word and the full stop is a closing quotation mark (but only in certain instances. See the chapter on QUOTATION MARKS).

The full stop in quotations

Let us assume that someone utters a complete sentence, for instance:

I'm going back to the hotel to get changed.

When you want to write down the exact words that were said, followed by a reporting verb (that is, a phrase such as *she said, I replied, he retorted, they chorused,* etc.), you put the words spoken into quotations marks and replace the full stop by a comma:

'*I'm going back to the hotel to get changed,*' Sheila said.

'*She's gone back to the hotel to get changed,*' I told them.

The comma that replaces the original full stop is placed inside the quotation marks.

If the reporting verb comes before the quotation, the sentence ends with a single full stop, which is placed before the final quotation mark:

Sheila said, 'I'm going back to the hotel to get changed.'

Raising my voice to make myself heard above the traffic, I called out, 'Sheila's gone back to the hotel to get changed.'

Remember the general rule that there should only be one full stop in a sentence.

NOT
Brian whispered, 'I know a little place where it's much quieter.'.

but
Brian whispered, 'I know a little place where it's much quieter.'

For more information about punctuation in quotations, go to the chapter on QUOTATION MARKS.

The full stop in abbreviations

Full stops are becoming much less commonly used in abbreviations. Forms such as

U.S.A.

B.B.C.

and

Y.M.C.A.

may once have been the norm, but they now look distinctly old-fashioned in British English. (Full stops are more often retained in abbreviations of all types in American English.)

It is therefore perfectly proper to write:

UN

EU

WWF

DVLA

Let me hasten to add that it is not wrong to write B.B.C. instead of BBC, it is simply unnecessary, and now so out of fashion that inserting the full stops may actually disconcert your reader slightly. Imagine, for instance, inserting full stops into CD, DVD or LOL (lots of love)!

The tendency to omit full stops applies to abbreviations of all sorts. It covers not only abbreviations made up of the initial letters of the words in the full form and pronounced as a string of letters (as shown in the examples above), but also to acronyms (which are also made up of initial letters but are pronounced as words, as in *FIFA*, *AIDS* and *BUPA*), to shortenings of longer words (*Jan*, *Feb*, *Ave*, *Cert Ed* and *nem con*) and to abbreviations formed by removing one or more letters from inside a word (*Dr*, *Rd*, *Mrs*, *ft*). Likewise, it makes no difference whether the abbreviation in question consists entirely of upper-case or capital letters (*PVC*), lower-case or small letters (*mph*) or a mixture of the two (*Mr*, *DfEE*).

I have said that it is not wrong to put in full stops (though in many cases it may look quaint); I have also said that it is not wrong to omit full stops. You may conclude from this that there are no rules for putting full stops into abbreviations, or that the only rules are ones that you make up for yourself. You would be essentially correct in coming to this conclusion. My personal feeling, for what it is worth, is that full stops in abbreviations are nowadays a waste of space. Rather than make life complicated for yourself, leave them out. It shows no disrespect to J K Rowling, for example, to write her name that way, rather than as J.K. Rowling, and between 30p and 30p. there is not a penny either way.

By no means everyone, however, shares this opinion. Many people will happily write *NATO*, *DNA*, *MP* and *mph* (there are entries for all these terms in these exact forms in my copy of *The New Oxford Dictionary of English*), but jib at writing, for example:

eg for *e.g.* (*exempli gratia* or 'for example')

or

am for *a.m.* (*ante meridiem* or 'before noon')

or

Inc for *Inc.* (*incorporated*)

My copy of the first edition of *The New Oxford Dictionary* (published in 1998) gives all these terms with full stops. My slightly later copy of *Collins English Dictionary, 21st Century Edition* (published in 2001) has entries for:

e.g., **eg**, *or* **eg.**

a.m., **A.M.**, **am**, *or* **AM**

and for

Inc. *or* **inc.**

We usually go to dictionaries for authoritative advice on these matters. The entries from *Collins* show just how fluid the situation is with regard to abbreviations. Whereas, a few years ago, you might have had to find good reasons for leaving the full stops out, we have now probably reached a situation where the position is reversed, and you may have to find good reasons for keeping them in.

The reasons you might offer include the following:

Tradition – it has been traditional to put full stops in abbreviations, especially those that actually abbreviate Latin phrases such as *e.g.*, *i.e.* (*id est* or 'that is') or *nem. con.* (*nemine contradicente* or 'with no-one dissenting', hence 'unanimously'). People who started reading in the last century (still, at the time of writing, the majority of the population) are used to seeing these abbreviations with full stops in them. To many people, they look wrong with the full stops left out.

Clarity – when written without full stops, some abbreviations have the same form as actual words, *a.m* being a classic example. If you write *1 am*, people may read it as *I am*; if you write *1am* people may read it as *lam* (you are, admittedly, rather safer after one o'clock in the morning). If you write *f.o.b.*, everyone will know at once that you are using an abbreviation (meaning 'free on board'). If you write *fob*, they may think you mean 'a watch chain', 'an ornament attached to a watch chain' or 'a pocket for a watch'. Finally, *no. 13* offers no possibility of confusion, while the same cannot be said of *no 13*, and you might conceivably find yourself writing *There is no no 13 in this street*.

The rule(s) – I personally know of only one rule that many publishers and individuals apply fairly systematically. That rule is that where a contraction (a shortened form of a word) does not end with the final letter of the full form of the word, you should close it with a full stop. When, for instance, you shorten the word *etcetera* to *etc.*, you need the full stop because the abbreviated form does not end with the letter *a*. On the basis of this rule, *Inc.* (short for Incorporated) requires a full stop because it does not end with a *d*, but *Ltd* (short for Limited) does not. Similarly, the abbreviation *Jan.* (for January) gets a full stop, but the abbreviation *yr* (year) does not; *Mr*, *Mrs* and *Dr* are correctly written without a full stop, but *Prof.*, *Col.* and *Rev.* are not.

Before we proceed further and attempt to reach a conclusion about the correct way of showing abbreviations, let me make three important points.

Any full stops that you use at the end of abbreviations form an exception to the general rule that sentences should not contain more than one full stop:

> She worked for Apex Ltd of Leeds, Acme Inc. of Trenton, New Jersey, and Jones & Co. of Cardiff before coming to us.

When the last word in the sentence is an abbreviation with a full stop, however, you should not put in another full stop:

> Her last job was with Jones & Co.

> NOT
> Her last job was with Jones & Co..

But you can put any other punctuation mark after the full stop that closes an abbreviation:

> You'll be doing all the usual kinds of office work: typing, filing, organising, etc., etc., etc.

> Was your last job with Jones & Co.?

> I resigned from Acme Inc.; it was probably the best decision I ever made.

Abbreviations and style

In the previous section, I put forward the opinion that it is probably better nowadays to dispense with full stops after abbreviations. I certainly cannot present that as a rule. It is simply a suggestion based on current trends and a fluid situation. While I have a good deal of sympathy with people who cannot bring themselves to write *eg, 7 am* etc, I do not think that tradition is really good enough grounds for preserving something that is not strictly necessary; I do not think clarity is an issue in most cases, because it should be perfectly obvious from the contexts when you are, for instance, talking about old-fashioned watches and watch chains, and when you are talking about conditions for the delivery of goods; and finally, the rule about contractions is as often honoured in the breach as in the observance. According to the *Collins English Dictionary*, the abbreviation *St* means 'saint', but the abbreviation *St.* means 'street'. Since the word *street* also ends with a *t*, how is one supposed to know that, in this instance, the contraction consists of the first and second letters, not the first and final letters? Similarly, *Collins* gives *Cambs* and *Herts* without full stops for *Cambridgeshire* and *Hertfordshire*, respectively. This, surely, goes against the rule. Ironically perhaps, your best chance of maintaining consistency is, in fact, to drop all full stops after abbreviations.

It is easier to find more solid and less contentious ground, if we move the discussion briefly to questions of style. Here there are two main points to be made.

Whatever you choose to do with abbreviations, do it consistently. If you choose to write *e.g.* and *p.m.* on the first page, try to ensure that you are still using those same forms on the last page.

Beware of using too many abbreviations, especially in writing that is fairly formal or addressed to a wide readership, for two reasons. First, a great many modern documents, especially official, business and technical documents, bristle with sets of initials. These often look like a secret code; indeed, they often function like one for people who are not in the know. If you use abbreviations, make sure that you explain any that ordinary lay people may not be familiar with:

> *IDP (integrated data processing) is not a feature of this system.*

And second, e-mails, text messages and scrawled notes and memoranda are facts of modern life and very useful. Abbreviations of all sorts come in handy as methods of saving time and money in communications that are ephemeral, written in a hurry and often intended as parts of an ongoing conversation. However, if you are writing something that will appear on paper as opposed to on a screen, and that you would like to continue to read well and look good after a period of time, then it is better to avoid any short-cuts, including abbreviations. Writing things out in full also, incidentally, gets you round the problem of whether to use full stops with the abbreviations.

> *'There is no number thirteen in this street!' he exclaimed.*

> *I don't particularly like being woken up at five o'clock in the morning.*

> *With your legal training, there are many fields in which you could find a job besides the law itself: for example, in banking, insurance or commerce.*

The full stop in e-mail addresses

Full stops frequently appear in e-mail addresses; so do many other punctuation marks. It is probably not worth trying to think of any of them as punctuation marks in the ordinary sense. Nobody refers you to 'funnybunnies – full stop – co – full stop – uk'. Likewise, nobody giving dictation says 'Thank you for your letter – dot, capital letter – Is that your last word on the matter – question mark'. In e-mail addresses, a full stop is a dot, and the only thing you can really say about it is, that if you leave one out or put it in the wrong place, your e-mail will go astray.

A row of full stops

Three full stops one after the other form a special punctuation mark called an 'ellipsis' or an 'omission mark'. For a discussion of this form, please go to the chapter on THE ELLIPSIS.

Recap

- A full stop is used at the end of a sentence that is not a question or an exclamation.

- A full stop should not, as a rule, be used to close a set of words that do not form a proper sentence.

- There should not be more than one full stop at the end of a sentence.

- A full stop should only appear inside a sentence if it is attached to an abbreviation.

- Full stops have traditionally been used in many abbreviations, especially contractions of words that do not end with the final letter of the full form.

Exercise

Divide this passage up into proper sentences by inserting full stops (and putting capital letters in the appropriate places):

I can't remember exactly when it was that I last saw her it was a long time ago I know that because I remember talking to her about what she was going to do when she left school we were quite close in those days that changed when she left home and went to university there she found other friends and forgot about the people back home it seems to happen like that very often it's probably my fault for getting old

The Question Mark (?)

The basics

When do you use a question mark? The obvious answer is the correct one: at the end of a question.

You will not need me to tell you how to recognise an ordinary question. The word order in a statement, with the subject before the verb, is reversed. The statement

Dinner is ready.

becomes the question

Is dinner ready?

However, a set of words does not have to follow this standard pattern in order to be a question. When we are speaking to someone, we do not always bother to reverse the word order. Instead, we show that what we are saying is meant as a question by moving our voice to a slightly higher pitch (going up) at the end of the sentence. There is no way of showing this in writing except by adding a question mark:

You made it all by yourself?

That was your first attempt?

In fact, in writing, you can make almost anything that is addressed to someone (including yourself or the reader) into a question simply by adding a question mark:

> *Surely you don't believe that one single person was responsible for literally hundreds of crimes committed all over the country?*

although in both speech and writing we often reinforce the sense that something is a question by adding a little tag at the end:

> *Surely you don't believe that one single person was responsible for literally hundreds of crimes committed all over the country, do you?*

There are not a great many complications or difficulties in using the question mark, but let us begin our coverage of its few peculiarities by looking at these tags.

Question tags and tag questions

Question tags are little phrases such as *do you?, can he?, have we?* or *isn't it?* In all of them the verb comes before the subject, so that, on their own, they constitute short two-word questions of the ordinary kind. We can make a statement addressed to another person into a question by raising the pitch of our voice when speaking, or by adding a question mark when writing. Adding a question tag, however, makes it much more obvious that we are putting a question and, usually, expect a reply. A question formed by adding a tag is called a tag question:

> *He can't seriously be intending to resign, can he?*

> *So you'll organise the hiring of the coach, will you?*

> *This is your first attempt at making a cake, isn't it?*

It is important to remember that the verb in the tag must match the verb in the main part of the sentence:

NOT
He can't seriously be intending to resign, will he?

When the verb in the main part of the sentence is in the negative (that is, accompanied by *not*), the verb in the tag must be positive:

He can't seriously be intending to resign, can he?

This isn't your first attempt at making a cake, is it?

But when the verb in the main part of the sentence is positive, the verb in the tag can be either positive or negative:

This is your first attempt at making a cake, isn't it?

This is your first attempt at making a cake, is it?

Adding a negative or positive makes a slight difference to the way the sentence should be spoken and to its overall tone.

These particular issues relate to grammar rather than punctuation. They do have a bearing on punctuation, however, if only because tag questions, by convention, always end with a question mark, even though the question mark sometimes 'feels wrong'.

We do not need much experience of ordinary conversation to know that sentences of this kind are often not really questions at all. Frequently, they are statements or commands masquerading as questions.

You can, for instance, say the words:

> *This is the way to the station, isn't it?*

in a way that suggests that you are very unsure about how to get to the station. But you can also say them in a way that suggests you jolly well know it's the way to the station and will be very upset if someone tells you the station is in the completely opposite direction:

> *This is the way to the station, isn't it(, my good man)?*

When you say those words in that tone, your voice does not go up on the very last word of the sentence as it does in an ordinary question. Instead you emphasise the one-from-last word, *isn't,* just as you do when you say:

> *It's lovely weather for the time of the year, isn't it?*

> *You can't take it with you when you die, can you?*

> *If that's his attitude, he mustn't be surprised if people don't like him, must he?*

There simply is no special punctuation mark that covers utterances of this kind. Whatever their tone, and whatever the intentions behind them, these remarks count as questions and must be closed with question marks.

Question marks in quotations

When you write down the exact words used by somebody else when asking a question, those words should end with a question mark, and the question mark should be placed inside the quotation marks:

> *'Where are you going?' he asked.*

> *He looked me straight in the eye and said, 'Is that really the whole truth?'*

There is no need for a comma after the question mark or the closing quotation mark in the first example. Nor is a full stop necessary after the question mark or the closing quotation mark in the second. A question mark, remember, is a standard way of closing a sentence and does not need to be reinforced by a full stop.

If you quote someone else's words in a question of your own, however, the question mark comes outside the quotation marks:

> *Do you happen to know who said, 'I think therefore I am'?*

> *Is there really any future for what he calls 'public-private relationships'?*

It probably will not happen very often, but if you wish to quote a question inside and at the end of another question, you will need question marks both before and after the closing quotation mark:

> *Aren't you fed up with hearing them repeat the same old question, 'When will we get there?'?*

> *Did I hear you calling out, 'Who's got my tennis racket?'?*

It is usually possible to rephrase the sentence in some way so as to avoid the string of punctuation marks at the end:

> *Aren't you fed with hearing them ask when they will get there?*

> *Did I hear you calling out to ask who's got your tennis racket?*

Indirect questions

What we did at the end of the last section in order to get round the slight awkwardness of having two question marks was to change a direct question into an indirect one.

A direct question is one that is, in the broadest sense, addressed to somebody. (That somebody may be yourself, your reader, every-one within earshot or nobody in particular.)

> *'Has anyone seen my tennis racket?'*

is a direct question;

> *'Has anyone seen my tennis racket?' she called out.*

is a sentence that quotes this direct question and uses a reporting verb to attribute it to someone;

> *She asked if anyone had seen her tennis racket.*

turns the direct question into an indirect one by replacing the words that were actually spoken by other words that convey the same meaning.

Indirect questions are one example of a broader phenomenon called 'indirect speech' or 'reported speech'. This is a process in which you put the words that someone actually says into a slightly different form (sometimes changing the personal pronoun and the tense of the verb).

> *'I'm very happy here.'*

is direct speech;

> *She says (that) she is very happy here.*

is indirect speech.

You do not need to put indirect speech into quotation marks, because you are not reproducing the exact words that the person spoke. More important for our immediate purposes, however, is the fact that you normally do not need to close an indirect question with a question mark.

> *Are you going out tonight?*

but

> *He asked if I was going out tonight.*

or

> *He asked her whether she was going out tonight.*

Likewise:

> *When are you coming?*

but

> *He asked (me) when I was coming.*

The majority of indirect questions are prefaced by one or other form of the verb *to ask* and either *if* or *whether* or the question word used in the original enquiry. But it is not obligatory to use *ask*:

> *They were trying to find out if the goods they ordered had arrived.*

> *We've had hundreds of people enquiring when the new model will be available.*

> *She wanted to know how my sister was doing.*

The general rule to remember is that indirect questions do not take a question mark. However, there are two exceptions to this rule. The first is when the indirect question forms part of a direct question:

> *Why are you asking me whether you should go or not?*

> *Can anyone tell me whose suitcase this is?*

The second is when a statement containing an indirect question is phrased in a very tentative way, suggesting that the speaker is too polite or too unsure of himself or herself to ask for something outright, and, so to speak, disguises a direct question as an indirect one. These statements frequently open with the verb *wonder*. It is customary to close them with a question mark:

> *I was wondering if you could possibly help me?*

> *We were wondering if those seats were taken?*

Perhaps you would be so kind as to ask your sister if she still has my book?

Statement or question?

It is sometimes difficult to decide whether sentences that contain the word *question* itself should end with a question mark or not. The following examples illustrate the difficulty:

The question that everyone is asking is who is going to be the next prime minister.

The question is not whether we can do it, but how we do it and when.

We must look again at the question of where our real strengths lie.

You may feel tempted to put a question mark at the end of these sentences, particularly the first one, but the temptation should be resisted. In all these instances, you are not actually asking the questions involved, but saying what the questions are. These are statements therefore and must end with full stops.

It does, admittedly, seem rather tame to end the first example without a question mark, since anyone of a dramatic disposition would be inclined to pause in the middle of the sentence:

The question that everyone is asking is . . .

You could inject a bit more drama into the sentence, however, by turning the last part into a quotation, which would entitle you to use a question mark:

The question that everyone is asking is, 'Who is going to be the next prime minister?'

Indicating uncertainty

A question mark, sometimes enclosed in round brackets (?), is also used before or after something in a passage of text that is not known for certain to be true, for instance a figure or a date:

William Langland (?1330–?1400) is perhaps the most important poet of fourteenth-century England apart from Geoffrey Chaucer.

Her name is Kathryn (?) – I'm not sure that that's the right spelling.

Recap

- A question mark indicates that a sentence is to be understood as a question, whether or not the usual order of subject and verb is reversed.

- A direct question always ends with a question mark.

- An indirect question does not end with a question mark unless it is part of a sentence that is constructed as a question or phrased in a very tentative way.

- A question mark can indicate that the accuracy of a piece of information is uncertain.

Exercise

Decide which of these sentences should end with a question mark and which with a full stop:

1) *Did you or did you not remove the papers from the folder*

2) *The question now is where do we go from here*

3) *There were always likely to be difficulties, weren't there*

4) *I'm not leaving until you tell me whether it's true or not*

5) *I wonder if I might ask you a question*

Insert the full stops, question marks and capital letters necessary to make this passage read satisfactorily:

I really didn't have a clue what he was talking about and wondered whether he had completely lost his mind is there such a thing as juvenile dementia could it be that he was on drugs was it simply that I had completely lost touch with the way that young people think and express themselves I had never asked myself whether my own ability to communicate might be at fault the question of whether it might not be began to loom large in my mind

The Exclamation Mark

The basics

Thank heaven for the exclamation mark! Lively, mischievous and tongue-in-cheek writers would be lost without it.

In sober prose, however, the exclamation mark is probably the least common of the three possible ways to close a sentence – perhaps because it is not an entirely sober symbol! It generally indicates that someone is in the grip of a powerful feeling such as anger or surprise and is therefore expressing himself or herself with unusual forcefulness. Moreover, the use of the exclamation mark is often at the writer's discretion. By and large, the rules of grammar and sentence construction determine whether your sentences close with full stops or question marks. But, although there are rules that apply to the exclamation mark, it is your feeling for language and for the situation in which particular words are being used that mainly dictates where and when you put one in. The question mark, as we have already seen, can be used to indicate tone, that is, to convey a particular kind of emotion or attitude in the speaker above and beyond the meaning of the words he or she actually uses. The exclamation mark is much more decidedly an indicator of tone, and tone is or should be very much under the writer's control.

Let me try to illustrate this point. By closing the same set of words with a different punctuation mark, we immediately change their tone, that is, we change the way that the reader imagines them to have been spoken.

You walked home alone.

Closed with a full stop, these words seem almost completely unemotional. As they stand, on their own, there is nothing really for the reader's imagination to latch on to. We have no idea when or why they were said.

You walked home alone?

Once we replace the full stop with a question mark, things start to happen. The reader knows that more than one person is involved, because this is not the kind of question you put to yourself or to nobody in particular. The reader will also instinctively, I feel, try to imagine the tone in which this question could be asked. It might be asked noncommittally; it might be asked very suspiciously; it might even be asked in a tone of amazed admiration. Four words and a question mark do not take the reader very far, in the absence of any other context, but there is something for the imagination to work on, and what has made the difference is the change in punctuation because the words themselves remain the same.

You walked home alone!

Replacing the original full stop with an exclamation mark has an even more powerful effect. Understood as an exclamation and therefore as having considerable force behind them, these four simple words acquire a much stronger and, I think, more specific emotional charge. It is difficult *not* to imagine them being uttered by someone who is anxious about or angry with another person, and the reader's natural assumption is that this other person ran some sort of risk by walking home alone – or at least that the speaker believed that was the case. A little scenario has been created: again, largely by the punctuation.

While I hope that this little exercise has reinforced the idea that punctuation can be used creatively, its main purpose has been to provide a brief introduction to the potential of the exclamation mark. It is a pretty powerful tool. You can do a lot with it. But, like all powerful things, it sometimes needs to be handled with restraint.

Now let us deal with the circumstances in which the exclamation mark is the correct way to close a sentence.

Exclamations

An exclamation mark, naturally enough, closes an exclamation. An exclamation is a sound or a word that a person utters forcefully, usually under some kind of emotional or physical stress. Exclamations are often very short, do not always consist of actual words and may not constitute a standard sentence:

> *Ugh!*
>
> *Ow!*
>
> *Hey!*
>
> *Help!*
>
> *Damn!*
>
> *Fire!*
>
> *Police!*

By no means all one-word sentences require an exclamation mark, but many of them do. Likewise not all exclamations consist of a single word:

What a lovely surprise!

How beautiful she looks in that dress!

Now that's what I call a cigar!

You bastard! You rotten, stinking bastard!

I don't believe it!

Some of these examples are conventional sentences and some are not, but they all express a strong emotion forcing its way out and that is what makes them exclamations.

Since it is the emotional charge that basically makes the exclamation, an exclamation mark can sometimes be used in place of a question mark, when a question is put in an exclamatory way:

Won't somebody help me!

Isn't it just the most beautiful thing you ever saw!

Why can't I be like Janet!

It is sometimes a matter of fine judgement to decide whether a question mark or an exclamation mark is more appropriate. Again, your sense of the emotional pressure behind the question is the deciding factor. Sometimes people put a question mark and an exclamation mark together at the end of such an outburst:

Did you ever see such a mess?!

but this is unnecessary. The exclamation mark is correct on its own.

Like questions, commands can be delivered with varying degrees of force. A command uttered in a mild tone of voice should end with a full stop:

> *Don't touch, there's a good boy.*
>
> *Keep off the grass, please.*
>
> *Look before you cross the road.*
>
> *Pass me the salt.*

But when a command is screamed, shouted, or spoken with great urgency, it should end with an exclamation mark.

> *Don't touch me!*
>
> *Keep you hands off!*
>
> *Watch out!*
>
> *Nobody move!*

When you quote an exclamation, the exclamation mark comes inside the quotation marks:

> *'Long life to the happy couple!' they chorused.*
>
> *'Well, blow me down!' he exclaimed.*

Noises off

Exclamation marks are also usually placed after words that indicate loud sounds, when those words are used in isolation:

> *Bang! There was a loud explosion and people started running in all directions.*

> *The pile of plates swayed and tottered, then – crash! – it fell to the floor.*

You do not, of course, need an exclamation mark when a word like *bang* or *crash* is used inside an ordinary sentence:

> *The plates fell with a crash to the floor.*

Exclamation marks and humour

In informal pieces of writing, such as letters or e-mails to friends, or when writers are trying to reproduce conversation on paper, the exclamation mark is often used to show that something is meant humorously or ironically:

> *We've all heard about Donald's famous complaint, of course!*

> *As usual, I was delighted to receive their ten-page Christmas round-robin and hear all about the hamster's medical history!*

> *Bella's dress was not so much revealing as exhibitionistic, if you know what I mean!*

> *'I know she's not referring to me', said Frank, 'because*
> *I'm the very model of good behaviour!'*

Needless to say, you should use exclamation marks sparingly, if at all, in more formal and sober pieces of writing such as business letters and reports. Similarly, the use of multiple exclamation marks:

> *It was big! It was huge!! It was e-nor-mous!!!*

should be kept for very informal or comic writing.

Some perhaps excessively strait-laced or high-minded people frown on the use of the exclamation mark in written communications of any kind. If you pepper a letter, say, with exclamation marks, it does tend to suggest that you were jumping up and down in your seat as you wrote it. Your reader may be in a different mood and not altogether receptive to a tone of high excitement when he or she tries to take in what you have to say. Nevertheless, used correctly and not too frequently, the exclamation mark adds excitement, creates drama and can bring to black and white letters on a page some of the colourfulness of emotional speech.

Recap

- An exclamation mark offers an alternative to the full stop and the question mark as a way of closing a sentence.

- To qualify for an exclamation mark, an utterance or sentence should be produced under pressure or contain a strong emotional charge.

- When you place an exclamation mark at the end of a sentence, you indicate that it is not to be read or understood as being in a flat unemotional tone.

- You can use an exclamation mark at the end of a question, if the question is an exclamatory one.

- Exclamation marks can also be used to indicate that a remark is intended humorously or ironically.

- Exclamation marks should not be overused, especially in serious writing.

Exercise

Put exclamation marks at the end of the sentences that seem to need them (and use question marks or full stops for the others):

1) *What a beautiful day for a picnic*

2) *Can I help you with anything*

3) *She never stops talking for a minute*

4) *Splash the little dog leapt into the water to fetch the stick*

5) *Why didn't you tell me the gun was loaded*

6) *Get out of here this minute*

Insert full stops, question marks, exclamation marks and capital letters in the appropriate places in this passage:

'The war's over' people were running out into the streets shouting the good news to their neighbours what a relief there would be no more dreading the postman's arrival in case he brought bad news there would be no more shortages and belt-tightening either who could doubt that things were about to get better there was plenty to recover from, but recovery would be swift, wouldn't it of course it would the war was over hurrah

2 Punctuation inside the sentence

The comma

The basics

Despite being such a small and insignificant-looking little thing, the comma has a great variety of uses. It also has a very important role to play in preserving the difference between sense and nonsense in what we write. It is probably the most popular punctuation mark – at least for use inside sentences. People may deny any knowledge of the colon and semicolon and say they never put one in. Nobody, to my knowledge, claims total ignorance of the comma. Consequently, it tends to be used rather a lot – sometimes where a colon or semicolon ought to be.

Reliance on the comma is in keeping with the general trend in modern English writing, which is to punctuate lightly. Instead of breaking up the flow of the sentence with 'heavy' stops (like the colon and the semicolon), modern writers prefer, on the whole, to keep order with a gentle touch, using commas. A comma indicates only a slight pause – if, indeed, it indicates a pause at all. Nevertheless, its correct use is governed by a fairly complex set of rules, so this will be quite a 'heavy' section.

Most of us are probably introduced to the comma as a linker. When schoolchildren have learnt to begin sentences with capital letters and end them with full stops, the next stage in their progress is to grasp that you do not have to put each separate piece of information in a separate sentence. You can put two or more pieces of information together and link them with *and*. So,

> *We had juice. We had sandwiches. We had biscuits. We had a big cake.*

becomes

> *We had juice and we had sandwiches and we had biscuits and we had a big cake.*

At this point the stage is set for the entrance of the comma. The teacher can then point out that this clever little piece of punctuation enables you to avoid using *and* all the time. Indeed, it can replace the three words *and we had*, so that the big long sentence with three *ands* can be whittled down to:

> *We had juice, sandwiches, biscuits and a big cake.*

The teacher might even take this opportunity to introduce a useful rule, which is that you can, in many cases, check whether you have put a comma in the correct place by reversing the initial process and reinserting an *and* in place of a comma. If putting back *and* does not alter the sense of what you have written or reduce it to nonsense, this is a pretty sure sign that your comma is correctly positioned. We shall call this 'the *and* test'.

Insofar as it can replace *and* and the other main linking word *or*, the comma can usefully and conveniently be thought of as a 'linker'. It can be used, in conjunction with *and*, *or* or *but*, to join two main clauses together; it can also be used to attach a subordinate clause to the main clause.

However, you can only go so far with the idea of the comma as a linker. Like the other punctuation marks that appear inside the sentence, it indicates a pause, albeit a slight one, and it is perhaps debatable whether a pause sign can really act as link. What is quite certain, however, is that, in much of the work that it does, the comma acts as a 'separator'. It marks off a word, or a group of words, from the rest of the sentence.

Except at the beginnings or ends of the sentence, separating commas tend to work in pairs. This is a vital point to remember. If you are going to mark off a section of text, the reader will want to know exactly where it begins and where it ends. If you put in one comma and omit to put in another, the reader will carry on to the end of the sentence and assume that everything between the comma and the final full stop, question mark or exclamation mark is a viable section. If a second comma is actually necessary, the result will be nonsense:

> *We can't, however absolutely guarantee that.*

> *It's just, as I said that Myrtle won't like it.*

If you add another comma to mark the end of the section, sense is restored:

> *We can't, however, absolutely guarantee that.*

> *It's just, as I said, that Myrtle won't like it.*

Remember the rule: in the middles of sentences, commas work in pairs.

You can easily check whether you have enough commas and that they are in the right places. Generally speaking, the piece of text marked off is an 'optional extra' in the basic sentence. It is additional to it and also, up to a point, dispensable: you can remove it without destroying the sentence completely. The basic test for the correct use of separator commas is to imagine away the words between the first comma and the next punctuation mark and see what you are left with. If what remains still makes good sense and conveys the necessary information, you have got your comma or commas right. This procedure will be referred to as 'the removability test'.

If we subject two of the examples given above to this test, we get:

> *We can't . . .*

which is obviously unsatisfactory, or:

> *We can't . . . absolutely guarantee that.*

which is fine.

Now, having established a basic framework, let us look in detail at the use of the comma as linker and separator.

The comma as linker

The comma in lists

As the teacher pointed out, commas are used to link together the items in lists:

> *We stopped over on the way in Geneva, Milan and Venice.*

> *The pupils have to opt for tennis, badminton, volleyball or netball.*

Peter, John, Tom and Paul are all coming.

The items in the lists need not all be single words:

> *The Red Lion, the Cat and Fiddle, the Queen's Head and the Hope and Anchor are all within staggering distance of one another.*

> *We've invited Percy's mother, Brian's brother and sister, Jane's uncle and aunt and Charlotte's niece.*

Commas can also be used to link a series of clauses:

> *It's up to you when you do it, where you do it, how you do it and whether you get anyone to help you.*

> *I pointed out that the wing was dented, there was a crack in the windscreen, one of the door handles was missing and one of the tyres was flat.*

> *She protested that it was all a terrible mistake, that she had intended to pay for the goods and that she had been as surprised as everyone else when the alarm went off.*

You will notice that the words, phrases and clauses separated by the commas are all of the same type. This is an important point that I will elaborate on later.

The serial comma

You will notice also that in all the example sentences given above there is one comma fewer than there are items in the list. There is no comma before the *and* or *or* that introduces the final item. It is not a rule that this should be so, but most writers in Britain follow this practice.

However, it is perfectly permissible to insert a final comma before *and* or *or*.

> *The colours of the French tricolour are blue, white, and red.*

> *He was obviously either drunk, demented, or both.*

The additional comma is generally known as the 'serial comma' (or occasionally in Britain as the 'Oxford comma'). It is the general practice in America to use the serial comma. Many British writers use it too. It has the advantage of preventing any possibility of the last two items in a list being run together:

> *The items on the menu included fish and chips, bubble and squeak, steak and kidney pudding and tripe and onions.*

If you are familiar with the glories of English cooking, you will not be expecting the restaurant to be offering combinations of steak and kidney and tripe and onions, or even of pudding and tripe. If you are unfamiliar with either the English language or English cuisine, such a sentence may leave you feeling rather bewildered. The addition of an extra comma makes everything crystal clear:

> *The items on the menu included fish and chips, bubble and squeak, steak and kidney pudding, and tripe and onions.*

When you start to write something, you should decide whether you are going to use the serial comma or not (this book does not). However, if you choose to do without the serial comma as a rule, you are perfectly entitled to put in the extra comma when it is required for clarity's sake.

Commas linking adjectives in front of nouns

Commas are also used to link a series of adjectives (that is, descriptive words such as *lovely, grey, sweet, wet, tall* and *short*) placed in front of the same noun:

> *a bunch of lovely, juicy, mouth-watering grapes*

> *a sweet, sickly and almost overpowering odour*

> *constantly wet, thoroughly vile and psychologically dispiriting weather*

> *the tall, glass-panelled, gherkin-shaped Swiss Re Building*

There are a few points to notice here.

First, the comma is thought of as replacing *and* just as it does in other types of list:

> *a bunch of lovely and juicy and mouth-watering grapes*

Consequently, you do not need a comma after the last adjective in the series because

> *a bunch of lovely and juicy and mouth-watering and grapes*

makes no sense.

Second, when the last two adjectives before the noun are already joined by *and*, you only need a comma in front of the *and* if you are using the serial comma, so that both

> *a sweet, sickly and almost overpowering odour*

and

> *a sweet, sickly, and almost overpowering odour*

are correct, but you should only use the second alternative if you are punctuating other types of list in the same way.

Third, as I mentioned a little earlier, commas should be used in lists to link words, phrases or clauses of the same type. In the examples we are using here, not all the descriptive words are adjectives. Some are adverbs (words such as *constantly* and *thoroughly* that generally end in *-ly* and are used, among other things, to describe adjectives in rather the same way that adjectives describe nouns):

> *constantly wet, thoroughly vile and psychologically dispiriting weather*

You should never put a comma between an adverb and the adjective it goes with: the weather is not *constantly and wet*, so it cannot be *constantly, wet* either. You can, however, link two or more adverbs describing the same adjective with commas in the normal way:

> *The weather was thoroughly, utterly and unspeakably vile.*

The fourth point follows on from points one and three. I have said that you should not put a comma between the last adjective in the list and the noun it relates to. That rule needs to be extended slightly: you should not put a comma between the final adjective and any word that is very closely bonded with the noun or actually forms part of it.

Let me refer back to one of our previous examples

> *the tall, glass-panelled, gherkin-shaped Swiss Re Building*

The so-called 'London Gherkin' is owned by a reinsurance company based in Switzerland and known as Swiss Re. Its more official name is the Swiss Re Building. The adjectives *tall, glass-panelled* and *gherkin-shaped* refer specifically to the Swiss Re Building, not to any old building. In this case, the adjective *Swiss* and the contraction *Re* are bonded with the noun *Building* to form the building's name. Consequently, it would be wrong to put a comma between *gherkin-shaped* and *Swiss*, although in other contexts *Swiss* can be used like any other adjective:

> *French, Swiss, Austrian and Italian ski resorts*

Let me give a more homely example of a noun consisting of a bonded pair of words: *swiss roll*. A *swiss roll* is not a roll that is Swiss as opposed to French or Italian, it is a thing in itself, so the two words together count as a noun. Therefore:

> *She offered me a slice of fresh-baked, home-made swiss roll.*

NOT
> *She offered me a slice of fresh-baked, home-made, swiss roll.*

This may seem like a rather finicky rule, but it is an important one since English possesses a great many two-word nouns (and a considerable number made up of three or more words). Moreover, it has long been the practice in English to treat nouns sometimes as if they were adjectives and use them to describe other nouns:

> *a mountain stream*
>
> *a duck pond*
>
> *a maternity hospital*

Mountain, duck and *maternity* are, of course, all nouns. Grammatically, they are in a different class from adjectives; therefore, they cannot be treated as if they were part of a list of adjectives:

> *This popular, local maternity hospital is now threatened with closure.*
>
> NOT
> *This popular, local, maternity hospital is now threatened with closure.*

and

> *I took a drink from a clear, cool, refreshing mountain stream.*
>
> NOT
> *I took a drink from a clear, cool, refreshing, mountain stream.*

Similarly, this sentence is correctly punctuated:

I took a drink of clear, cool, refreshing white wine.

This one is not:

I got a headache from drinking too much cheap, nasty, red wine.

Here we are talking about *white wine* and *red wine*, bonded concepts and two-word nouns. The final comma in the second example is, consequently, superfluous.

After this long and rather complicated explanation it may come as something of an anticlimax when I say that commas are not, in fact, obligatory in simple lists of adjectives before a noun. By simple lists, I mean lists in which all the describing words are adjectives and the noun is an ordinary 'unbonded' noun:

We walked along beside a muddy slow-moving stream.

With slow soft stealthy steps she stole along the corridor.

If there is any possibility of confusion, however, a comma (or some other punctuation mark) should be inserted:

a slow moving melody

Is the melody slow and moving or does it simply move slowly? If the former, the phrase needs a comma:

a slow, moving melody

if the latter, it needs a hyphen:

> *a slow-moving melody*

Let us now look at commas performing other types of linking work.

Commas linking main clauses

You can join two or more main clauses by a comma and a linking word such as *and, but* or *yet* instead of making them into two separate sentences:

> *He's in jail for breaking and entering, and now his wife's been arrested for shoplifting.*

> *There may be a simple explanation for all this, but we have so far been unable to find it.*

> *The lock is supposed to be childproof, yet it only took my children five minutes to find out how to open it.*

That is the general rule, but there are circumstances in which you do not need a comma. It is unnecessary (and incorrect) to use a comma when the subject is the same for both the verbs in the sentence:

> *She's been arrested for shoplifting and taken to the police station.*

(Compare this with the first of the previous set of examples where *he* is the subject of the first clause and *his wife*, the subject of the second.)

> *The car stopped and refused to start again.*

> *Snow will begin falling in Scotland during the morning and will move south as the day progresses.*

A comma can also be dispensed with, even if the two clauses have different subjects, when the clauses are relatively short and there is no natural break in the sentence.

> *My head was aching like fury and I had a very strange sensation in my stomach.*
>
> *She doesn't know but we do.*

If in doubt, however, put in a comma, because these sentences would not be incorrect if they had commas in them.

If you want to link two main clauses in the same sentence but do not want to use a co-ordinating conjunction such as *and*, you must use a semicolon (see THE SEMICOLON).

Commas linking subordinate clauses

A subordinate clause, as you may remember from the first section, is one that cannot function as a proper sentence on its own and usually opens with a conjunction such as *when, where, as, since, because* etc.

When a subordinate clause comes before the main clause, it is linked to it by means of a comma:

> *Before the game even started, there were several ugly incidents in the crowd.*
>
> *Since we're going to be here for some time, we might as well make ourselves comfortable.*

Because the wood was damp, I couldn't get it to light.

Although the price was right, there were several other things about the house that were wrong.

Subordinate clauses may also be linked by a comma when they follow the main clause. Commas are not always necessary, however, and in certain cases it is actually wrong to put one in.

You should not use a comma in front of a clause beginning with *that*:

He said that he would be here by eight.

NOT
He said, that he would be here by eight.

Similarly:

She was very surprised that you came.

It's true that we have very little in common.

However, remember that, if you have a series of clauses beginning with *that*, you can put commas between the second and third, third and fourth etc.

She protested that it was all a terrible mistake, that she had intended to pay for the goods and that she had been as surprised as everyone else when the alarm went off.

You should also not use a comma before a clause that explains the reason for what is stated in the main clause and so typically begins with *because*:

> He went to bed because he was tired out.
>
> NOT
> He went to bed, because he was tired out.

Similarly:

> You failed the exam because you didn't revise hard enough.
>
> I'm not missing a chance like this just because the weather's bad.

When a clause begins with *so* or *so that*, inserting a comma or leaving the comma out makes a difference to the meaning:

> I go to bed early so I can wake up early.
>
> I go to bed early, so I can wake up early.

The difference, unfortunately, does not immediately leap to the eye, but the first sentence, without the comma, expresses purpose: the speaker goes to bed early because he or she wants to wake up early. The second sentence expresses result: the speaker goes to bed early, and consequently he or she can wake up early in the morning. The difference can be seen more clearly in sentences that do not attempt to match each other exactly.

In the next two examples *so (that)* introduces a clause that expresses purpose and no comma is needed:

She is saving hard so she can go on holiday at the end of the year.

We came early so that we wouldn't have to queue.

However, in the next examples, *so (that)* introduces a clause that expresses result; a comma is, therefore, needed:

She has been saving hard, so she's got a lot of money in the bank.

We arrived early, so that we hardly had to queue at all.

It may be difficult sometimes to decide whether a clause of this type expresses purpose or result. Try a slightly different kind of *and* test. Insert an *and* in front of the *so* and ignore the *that* if there is one. If adding *and* does not change the meaning or create nonsense, you are dealing with a result clause:

We arrived early (and) so ~~that~~ we hardly had to queue at all.

But

We came early (and) so ~~that~~ we wouldn't have to queue.

makes no sense. This, therefore, is a purpose clause.

When other subordinate clauses follow the main clause, a comma is not usually necessary, but you may insert one when a slight pause fits the sense or the tone of the sentence.

I'll go when I'm good and ready.

She hasn't been the same since she had her accident.

I'd far rather discuss this later, when I've had time to think about it.

I will have a coffee then, since you insist.

In the first two sentences the latter part of the sentence runs on very naturally from the earlier part, so a comma would only get in the way. In the third, *later when I've had time to think about it* does not sound quite right; you would naturally break the sentence after *later* if you were saying it aloud. A comma is, therefore, in order. In the final sentence, the comma introduces a slight pause, which, to my mind, makes the final part of the sentence a little pointed.

Finally, if you wish to turn to turn a statement into a question by attaching a little question tag (*aren't I?, wasn't it?*) to the end of the sentence, you should always attach it with a comma:

You were with us on that occasion, weren't you?

It doesn't seem to make much difference, does it?

A comma replacing a verb

Occasionally, when you construct a sentence with two parts both of which use the same verb, you may find it neater to omit the second verb. If you choose to do that, you should replace the second verb with a comma.

He worshipped the ground she walked on; she worshipped the acres he owned.

could be transformed into:

> *He worshipped the ground she walked on; she, the acres*
> *he owned.*

From this rather literary usage, let us pass on to the other main function of the comma.

The comma as separator

As was pointed out in the introduction to this chapter, when commas act as separators, they generally work in pairs. However, a single comma will obviously suffice at the beginning or end of the sentence:

> *I should, nevertheless, like to be kept informed of any*
> *important developments.*

> *Nevertheless, I should like to be kept informed of any*
> *important developments.*

> *I should like to be kept informed of any important*
> *developments, nevertheless.*

Likewise, separating commas generally mark off a particular word or group of words that constitutes an addition, an 'optional extra', which can be removed without affecting the basic meaning of the sentence. Our discussions will centre on these removable additions, but there are two topics that I shall be considering separately: firstly, adverbs that are separated off by commas because they refer to the whole sentence and not to a particular part of it; secondly, relative clauses (clauses that begin with *who, which,* or *that* and describe or identify a person or thing). The presence or absence of commas around a relative clause affects the way in which we understand the relationship between the clause and the person or thing that it applies to.

Removable additions

Words such as *however, nevertheless, therefore* and *indeed* offer a comparatively easy way-in to this topic. They are frequently an addition to the sentences in which they occur, and there is no real problem with removing them:

> *I should, nevertheless, like to be kept informed of any important developments.*

> *I should . . . like to be kept informed of any important developments.*

While it may be quite clear that *nevertheless* can be taken out of the sentence without making it incomplete or nonsensical, it may not be quite so clear why it should be considered additional or optional. Let me try to clarify this point.

The real function of *nevertheless* and other words of the same kind is to link the sentence in which they appear to one that came before:

> *I don't expect you to give me hourly reports. I should, nevertheless, like to be kept informed of any important developments.*

Nevertheless is not a meaningless word, but there would actually be no point in putting it into the second sentence if the first sentence, or one that said something similar, were not there.

There are all sorts of other words that you could add to the sentence we are using as an example, but they would not be 'additional' in the sense that *nevertheless* is.

> *I should like to be kept regularly informed of any important developments*

> *I should very much like to be kept informed of any important developments.*

Regularly and *very much* are linked to *informed* and *like* respectively. They do not in any way take you outside the basic sentence. That, in a manner of speaking, is what *nevertheless* does. In our terms, that makes it 'additional' and also removable. As a result, it ought to be marked off by a comma or commas.

There are many words that perform a similar function and should generally be treated in the same way:

> *The government has, therefore, decided to take no action at this stage.*

> *We shall, notwithstanding, fulfil our side of the bargain.*

> *There can, however, be no real doubt about the nature of the threat we are facing.*

For a full understanding of what is being discussed in all these examples, you need to have heard or read what was said before. *Therefore, notwithstanding* and *however* also 'take you outside the sentence', so, within the sentence, they appear inside pairs of commas.

It is not only single words that perform this task, but also longer phrases.

> *There have been, as I was saying before, many similar cases in other countries.*

> *The death toll, according to these reports, now stands at three hundred.*

> *As a result, the rail service had to be suspended for several hours.*

Besides words and phrases that refer back to something mentioned earlier, there are others that indicate the attitude of the person speaking or writing it or offer a general comment on it:

> *To be honest, I don't really know what I ought to do.*

> *So, all things considered, it isn't such a bad result, is it?*

> *There are, in my opinion, no real losers under this arrangement.*

> *I think that, from our point of view, the sooner work gets started the better.*

> *That, I'm afraid, is all I have to give you.*

> *There are other ways of tackling the problem, you know.*

In all these examples – and they do not even come close to covering the whole range of such phrases, long and short – you have the sense of someone dropping in a little additional comment from outside the sentence. If you were reading these sentences aloud, you would probably pause fractionally at the points where the commas occur. If you remove the comments, the sentences survive. The commas are needed here and are doing their job effectively.

Sentence adverbs

Compare the two examples given below:

> *To travel hopefully is better than to arrive.*

> *My mother and sister will, hopefully, be arriving next week.*

In the first example, the adverb *hopefully* is linked with the words *To travel*. It describes the specific type of travel that is better than arriving. In the second example, *hopefully* is not linked to any particular word in the sentence; the speaker's mother and sister will not be arriving hopefully as opposed to dejectedly. Rather, *hopefully* relates to the sentence as a whole and expresses the speaker's feelings. It could be replaced by *I hope*, and some people think it ought to be, since using *hopefully* in this way is still frowned on in some quarters.

Because it relates to the sentence as a whole, *hopefully* is acting in the second example as what is called a 'sentence adverb'. Because it represents a kind of comment on the sentence, like the commenting phrases discussed in the previous section, it needs to be bracketed off with commas.

Here are two more pairs of examples that illustrate the same point:

He explained regretfully his reasons for not being able to attend.

I shall, regretfully, be unable to attend.

The industry seems inevitably doomed to decline.

The workers were, inevitably, the last people to be told what was happening.

It is, in the third example, apparently impossible for the industry to escape decline: it is *inevitably doomed*. The same adverb, however, functions differently in the fourth example. It would be perfectly possible for the workers to be informed at an earlier stage in the process, but the speaker or writer knows from experience that this is not the way things happen. *Inevitably* in the last example expresses that experience and the weary and rather cynical attitude that goes with it. It is a comment dropped in from outside and refers to the sentence as a whole. Therefore, it goes between commas.

Sentence adverbs are often paired with the word *enough*:

Funnily enough, that very same thought had just occurred to me too.

The woman I sat next to on the plane turned out, curiously enough, to be someone whom I had often contacted by e-mail but never met in person.

and the words *yes* and *no* and the phrase *thank you* are treated in exactly the same way:

Well, yes, I suppose you could say that.

No, I don't want one, thank you.

Now let us move on to deal with relative clauses.

The comma and relative clauses

A relative clause, as briefly described at the beginning of this section, begins with *who, which* or *that* and relates to a noun that it describes or defines in more detail.

> *I received a letter this morning from my aunt who lives in Nottingham.*
>
> *The book that you sent me was one that I had already read.*
>
> *The parcel, which had been posted on Saturday the 10th, did not arrive until Friday the 23rd.*

You will notice that in only one of these examples is the clause beginning with *who, which* or *that* enclosed in commas. There is a reason for this, but the removability test, which is normally a great help, does not really offer a clue to it, for

> *I received a letter this morning from my aunt.*

is certainly not nonsense or an imperfect sentence, any more than

> *The parcel did not arrive until Friday the 23rd.*

There are, in fact, two types of relative clause, and you have to be able to tell the difference between them in order to decide whether they need commas or not.

The first type is called a 'restrictive' or 'defining' relative clause, because it specifies or identifies what or who a particular thing or person is. A clause of this type is not enclosed in commas. The words 'restrictive' and 'defining' are not particularly illuminating on their own, so let me give some further examples:

> *My aunt who lives in Nottingham wrote to me this morning, but I haven't heard from my aunt who lives in Derby since last Christmas.*

> *The key that I keep in my desk drawer opens the safe; the key that is hanging on a hook in the kitchen opens the shed.*

We are talking about a particular aunt and a particular key (of at least two) in each case. Which one we are talking about is identified by the relative clause.

The second type is called a 'non-restrictive' or 'non-defining' clause. It simply provides a piece of additional information about the person or thing in question. To that extent, it is removable and, like all removable material, needs commas:

> *The suspect, who gave his name as Norman Ashworth, refused to answer any further questions.*

> *My car, which wasn't exactly new when I bought it, now looks like an absolute antique.*

Since the technical names given to these types of clause are pretty unhelpful, let us try to approach the distinction from another angle. It is largely a question of numbers.

The suspect, who gave his name as Norman Ashworth, refused to answer any further questions.

In the situation outlined in this sentence, there was only one suspect and the important thing about him is that he refused to answer any questions. He did volunteer that fact that his name was Norman Ashworth, but that is essentially by the by.

If we remove the commas we change the situation. The effect of using a defining clause about someone or something is to imply that there is more than one of them, just as in the previous examples there were two aunts and two keys. That is why you have to restrict your attention to a particular one of them and define which one you are talking about. To accommodate *the suspect* plus a defining clause properly, we would have to construct a sentence such as:

The suspect who gave his name as Norman Ashworth refused to answer any further questions, but the suspect who gave his name as Norman Unsworth sang like a canary.

Let me provide a few more sober example sentences containing defining clauses:

The man who rang the emergency services refused to give his name and address.

The copy that you gave me had several pages missing.

The film which we went to see last week is no longer showing.

There are many men, many copies and many films. It is the man who rang the emergency services, the copy that you gave, and the film which we went to see that, out of all the others, are the important ones.

Incidentally, the last of the most recent set of examples is generally acceptable in British English. But in American English, and among many careful writers of British English, *which* is only used to begin non-defining clauses; defining clauses begin with *that*. This is certainly a useful rule if it helps you to retain the distinction between the two types of clause:

> *The key that is on the hook in the kitchen and has a piece of yellow tape on it opens the shed.*

> *The key with the piece of yellow tape on it, which had been hanging on the hook in the kitchen when I went out, had mysteriously disappeared.*

Once again, in the first sentence the implication is that there are many keys, and we have to pick out the one to focus on. In the second sentence, we have already picked out one key and we provide an extra piece of information about it, which goes between commas.

When we have grasped the difference between the two types of relative clause, it becomes a fairly simple matter to deal with the use of commas in connection with people's names.

> *Mr David Jones, the company's vice president, gave a speech of welcome.*

> *Mr David Jones the baker usually plays the organ in chapel.*

In the first sentence, it is not absolutely necessary to identify which Mr David Jones gave the speech. In the second sentence, assumed to refer to a Welsh village where there may be several Mr David Joneses, it is deemed necessary to specify which one plays the organ, so the phrase *the baker* is not marked off by commas.

Compare the following:

> *The former England cricket captain Mike Gatting will be giving his analysis of the day's play.*

> *The team currently leading the Premiership, Manchester United, are at home today to Wigan.*

If you put Mike Gatting's name into commas, it would be removable, which would leave you with:

> *The former England cricket captain will be giving his analysis of the day's play.*

This is not nonsense, but on its own, since there are many former England cricket captains still with us, it is not very clear. But only one team can lead the Premiership at any one time; to that extent the identity of the team is incidental.

When you are actually addressing a particular person or particular people, however, you always put the name or the word that refers to them between commas.

> *Come over here, children, and see what I've found.*

> *Giles, what exactly do you think you are doing?*

> *Believe me, ladies and gentlemen, this is no laughing matter.*

I'm talking to you, Hoskins, so pay attention.

The reason why you should use commas when you mention the person or people you are actually speaking to should be clear from these examples:

I can't stop Sally. (Once she's made up her mind, there's no holding her back.)

I can't stop, Sally. (I'm in too much of a hurry.)

Commas and quotations

Commas have three main functions in quotations. First, they replace full stops inside the quotation marks, when you quote complete sentences and follow them with a reporting verb (*she said*, etc.):

'*I'm going back to the hotel to get changed,*' *Sheila said.*

'*She's gone back to the hotel to get changed,*' *I told them.*

Second, a pair of commas marks off the reporting verb when it is placed in the middle of the quotation:

'*I think*', *said Peter,* '*that there's something fishy going on.*'

'*Funnily enough,*' *she confided,* '*I was thinking exactly the same thing myself.*'

You will notice that in the first example, the first comma is placed outside the quotation marks, while in the second, it is placed inside the quotation marks. This is because of a general rule that says that punctuation that belongs with the words you quote goes inside the quotation marks, but punctuation that belongs with the main sentence goes outside them. The original sentences quoted were as follows:

I think that there's something fishy going on.

and

Funnily enough, I was thinking exactly the same thing myself.

The rule is that there is no comma before a clause beginning with *that*. The first comma in the first example is there simply to mark off the reporting verb; it, therefore, goes outside the quotation marks. *Funnily enough* is a sentence adverb. It should be followed by a comma. This comma belongs with the words quoted, so in the second example the first comma goes inside the quotation marks.

There is never any doubt, however, about where the second comma should go. It always goes immediately after the reporting verb or its subject and outside the second pair of quotation marks.

Third, a comma follows the reporting verb, even when no quoted words come before it:

She said, 'Let's go back to square one and start again.'

After puffing on his pipe for several seconds, he added, 'That seems like a good idea.'

For more on this topic, see QUOTATION MARKS.

Commas in numbers, dates and addresses

Commas have been traditionally used when you write out a figure with four or more digits (in other words the number one thousand or any larger number), grouping the digits in threes:

1,000

3,701,435

It is, however, increasingly common to find four-digit numbers without commas:

6479

The comma then makes an appearance only in numbers greater than ten thousand:

12,652

Commas are never used in numbers that refer to years:

the year 2007 NOT *2,007*

Generally, in British English, there is no need to insert commas into dates, unless you mention the day of the week

16 February 2007

February 16th 2007

Friday, February 16th 2007

It is standard American practice, however, to put a comma after the number of the day (which follows the name of the month).

August 19, 2005

The British Post Office is not keen on commas in addresses. You may put them at the end of every line of the address, but there is no need for them (or for a full stop at the end):

Arthur Clennam
The White House
12 Peabody St
Downminster Major
Gloucs
SN54 6TJ

Commas and meaning

As I said at the very beginning of this section, the comma plays a very important part in preserving the difference between sense and nonsense in what we write. If you forget to put in the second comma of a pair, which is easily done, confusion and unintentional humour often result. The same thing happens if you put a comma or commas in the wrong place.

Well, if you want my opinion it stinks.

This man is, as anyone can see really poorly.

> *The task is beyond me, and what is more, beyond the ability of any human being.*

The removability test (taking the words after the first comma, between two commas, or between the beginning of the sentence and the first comma out of the sentence, and seeing whether what is left makes sense) will generally set you right:

> *Well, . . .*

> *The man is . . .*

> *The task is beyond me . . . beyond the ability of any human being.*

Remember not to put a comma between the subject of a verb and the verb itself (often a temptation when you are using a lengthy relative clause), although you may put a phrase bracketed by commas in that position:

> *The man that you pointed out to me a moment ago, is leaving.*

> *. . . is leaving*

but

> *The man, whatever you think about his character and morals, is certainly a genius.*

> *The man . . . is certainly a genius.*

However, it is permissible to put in a comma if the same word would appear twice with nothing else in between:

What kind of noise it makes, makes no difference to me.

Finally, remember the dreadful warning contained in the title of Lynne Truss's famous book:

Eats, Shoots and Leaves

(although I have racked my brains for an alternative combination of words that would produce a similarly amusing and glaring instance of mispunctuation and not come up with one. This, hopefully, means that you are unlikely to fall into this particular trap too often.)

But why concentrate on the negatives? You can use the comma to adjust your meaning subtly. Here are three pairs of examples in which both sentences are correct, although they do not mean exactly the same thing:

There was bread and butter for those who wanted it.

There was bread, and butter for those who wanted it.

They were above all their closest rivals in the league.

They were, above all, their closest rivals in the league.

The people you know are the salt of the earth.

The people, you know, are the salt of the earth.

Recap

- The comma acts as both a linker and a separator.

- Commas are used to link the items in lists of words, phrases and clauses of the same type, usually replacing *and*. If the comma cannot be replaced by *and*, it is in the wrong place.

- There are two systems for using commas in lists: *A, B and C* and *A, B, and C*. The final comma in the second system is called the 'serial comma'.

- Commas, in conjunction with *and, or* or *but*, can link two main clauses.

- Commas also link subordinate clauses to the main clause.

- Commas acting as separators generally work in pairs, except when they are placed at the beginning or end of the sentence.

- Commas mark off words that are additional to the basic sentence.

- They also mark off sentence adverbs.

- Commas are not used with defining relative clauses (those in which the subject of the clause is one of a number of people or things of the same type).

- Commas are used with non-defining relative clauses (where the subject has already been identified and the clause gives additional information).

- Commas are used when you put the name of the person or people you are speaking to into your sentence.

- It is easy to misuse commas, but just as easy to use them effectively to get your exact meaning across.

Exercise

Put a comma, or commas, into the following sentences, if necessary:

1) *I put on my hat and coat and went out.*

2) *The professor however had other ideas.*

3) *After you've finished with the book can I borrow it?*

4) *I sharpened my pencil adjusted the desk lamp selected a fresh sheet of paper and prepared to write.*

5) *I've told you before that I don't have any money.*

6) *Jean who was waiting in the wings to go onstage got a fit of the giggles.*

7) *There isn't really time to do it now is there?*

8) *When we opened the door we found ourselves in a warm cosy comfortably furnished living room with a bright fire burning in the grate.*

9) *Comrades I have some bad news for you I'm afraid.*

10) *We don't generally discuss personal matters at committee meetings.*

Put in the commas, capital letters and other punctuation marks needed to make sense of this passage:

the woman that I love best in all the world is not generally speaking given to acting on impulse she considers things carefully and then carries out her plans slowly deliberately and methodically it takes her a long time to reach a decision but once the decision has been made she sticks to it as a result she seldom if ever makes a bad purchase if she does happen to choose unwisely however it takes a very long time to persuade her that she has done so I on the other hand tend to act on the spur of the moment I am the man for whom returns and refunds were invented because something that looks irresistible to me in the shop often looks irredeemable when I get it home opposites attract they say that must be how it is with us or we should have split up long ago

The colon (:)

The basics

The colon might loosely be called 'a suspender': it announces to the reader that what has just been said is not all that there is to say in this particular sentence. The words in front of a colon usually make up a statement that leaves something hanging in the air. The words that follow the colon end the suspense by adding to, explaining or clarifying whatever came before it.

The colon in lists

The colon can be seen performing its basic function most simply and clearly when it introduces a list:

I went into town to buy three things: a cassette for the printer, a pack of paper and a box of sticky labels.

She had all the qualities we were looking for: experience, good communication skills, plenty of personality and, above all, creative flair.

Please make a note of the things you will need to bring with you: a complete change of underclothing and a spare pair of socks; a stout pair of walking shoes or boots; a waterproof coat; a rucksack or any similar type of bag that you can carry on your back.

If you look carefully you will see that in all these examples, as in most other cases, the words that come before the colon could form a sentence on their own:

I went into town to buy three things.

Now, if at this point you simply want to go on with the story, you leave the full stop where it is:

I went into town to buy three things. Unfortunately, by the time I found somewhere to park I had forgotten what two of them were.

But if you want to add to, explain or clarify that opening statement – in this case to tell your reader exactly what those three things are – you need a different punctuation mark: the colon.

When you have put in a colon to mark the point at which your list begins, you need more punctuation to separate the various items in the list. In a relatively straightforward list commas will do this job quite adequately:

You will need the following ingredients for this recipe: 4 ounces of butter, 4 ounces of caster sugar, 6 ounces of self-raising flour, 2 eggs and a tablespoonful of milk.

But if you need a longer or more complicated phrase to describe one or more of the items – especially a phrase that has several commas in it – it is better to separate the items with semicolons:

There were three considerations that weighed particularly heavily with the committee: the contractor's inability to guarantee that the work would be completed on time; the fact that the original budget had already been exceeded; and the ongoing dispute with the union, which, according to the contractor, was

mainly responsible for the delays and the budget
overrun.

There is one final point that needs to be made before we look at the way the colon is used in other contexts. The colon should not, generally speaking, be used after the verb *to be* when you go on to give a list of ordinary nouns or noun phrases:

> *The three things to which I mainly owe my success are*
> *good sense, good health and good luck.*

> NOT
> *The three things to which I mainly owe my success are:*
> *good sense, good health and good luck.*

The colon breaks the sentence unnecessarily here and makes a fairly ordinary statement seem overdramatic. However, you could use a colon after *to be* if the second half of the sentence consisted of, for example, three verbs:

> *My grandmother lived by three simple rules, which*
> *were: don't drink or smoke; don't tell lies; do change*
> *your underwear at least once a week.*

The colon in ordinary sentences

Here is a different way of expressing the general rule that a colon introduces material that adds to, explains or clarifies what you say in the first part of your sentence.

When you use a colon to begin a list, you might say that it replaces the words *they are* or *they were*:

> *I went into town to buy three things. They were a cassette for the printer, a pack of paper and a box of sticky labels.*

When you use a colon in a sentence that does not contain a list, it can usually be thought of as replacing the words *which is (that)* or *that is to say (that)*:

> *I've got something really exciting to tell you: Jenny's expecting a baby.*

> *Read what it says on the label: you mustn't let the water boil away.*

> *He's a foreigner: he can't necessarily be expected to understand the British sense of humour.*

> *She's finally taken the plunge: she's starting up her own business.*

You could say:

> *I've got something really exciting to tell you, which is that Jenny's expecting a baby.*

It is not only neater, but also more dramatic, to use a colon instead.

The colon with extracts and quotations

You will probably have noticed that, throughout this book, colons have been used to introduce the examples. This is basically an extension of the use of a colon at the beginning of a list, but it is also

standard practice to use a colon to introduce anything that is 'extract-
ed' from your text, that is, written or printed after a blank line (and
often indented from the margin or shown in a different typeface):

> *I haven't yet come up with a definitive title for the book,
> but I thought that any of the following might do:*
>
> > *Two Returns to White Hart Lane*
>
> or
>
> > *Danny Blanchflower We Love You*
>
> or, more soberly,
>
> > *Memories of a Spurs Fan from the 1960s.*

Often the material in the extract will be a lengthy quotation:

> *George Eliot makes it quite clear at the beginning of
> Chapter 5 that there is nothing in her heroine's
> character to debar her from achieving social success:*
>
> > *Gwendolen's reception in the neighbourhood fulfilled
> > her uncle's expectation. From Brackenshaw Castle to
> > the Firs at Wanchester, where Mr Quallon the
> > banker kept a generous house, she was welcomed
> > with manifest admiration, and even those ladies
> > who did not quite like her, felt a comfort in having a
> > new, striking girl to invite.*

You can, however, use a colon to introduce a shorter quotation that you do not write out as an extract. But you only really need a colon if the words you quote follow the general rule and add to, explain or clarify what comes before it:

> *What he said sounded like a guess, but, if it was a guess, it was a good one: 'I'm not sure, but I think the answer's 37'.*

(For a fuller treatment of how to punctuate quotations, go to the chapter on QUOTATION MARKS.)

Specialised uses of the colon

A colon is also used between two numbers to indicate a ratio, for example when giving the odds in betting. One hundred to one can be shown as 100:1 and nine to two as 9:2. (In any kind of formal writing, however, it is better to write the ratio out in words.)

When you are writing a script for a play or film, you use a colon after the name of the character who is to speak a particular line:

Jane:	*Where are you taking me?*
The Ghost:	*That is for me to know, and you to guess at.*
Jane:	*I'm frightened.*

(The name followed by the colon is usually called a 'speech prefix'.)

You use a colon to divide the subtitle of a book or article from its main title:

Two Returns to White Hart Lane: Memories of a Spurs Fan in the 1960s

Putting a Girdle Round the Earth: a Geographer's Guide to Accurate Measurement.

You use a colon after words such as *to*, *from* or *re* in the headings of memos or business correspondence:

To: All members of staff.

From: The chairman.

Re: Timekeeping.

Colons and capital letters

In British usage it is not usually correct to use a capital letter after a colon in ordinary sentences. (It is perfectly correct, however, to use a capital letter after a colon in a title, a speech prefix or a heading.) In American usage a colon is often followed by a capital letter, especially when the section after the colon could form a complete sentence on its own:

There were only three things wrong with his performance: he looked wrong, he spoke too slowly and he bored everyone to death.

(British usage)

There were only three things wrong with his performance: He looked wrong, he spoke too slowly, and he bored everyone to death.

(American usage)

Recap

- A colon suspends a sentence. What follows the colon adds to, explains or clarifies what came in front of it.

- The colon is usually the correct punctuation mark to use if you could otherwise complete your sentence with a phrase beginning *they are, which is (that)* or *that is to say (that)*.

- The words that come before the colon should make up a complete sentence.

- Items listed after a colon should be separated by commas or semicolons.

- Colons are not followed by capital letters in British usage.

- Colons are also used in ratios, after speech prefixes and the introductory words to some headings, and before subtitles.

Exercise

Put a colon in the correct position in the following sentences (and add any other necessary punctuation):

1) *You made one fatal error you underestimated your opponent.*

2) *Four players miss this match because of injury Jones Lamb Hall and Myers.*

3) *My life with Matilda Higginbottom the autobiography of a hen-pecked husband.*

4) *If I die I want you to do one thing for me to make sure that Rover is well looked after.*

The semicolon (;)

The basics

A semicolon is stronger than a comma, but weaker than a full stop; it can generally be replaced by either of them; it is used to link two or more statements that could function as separate sentences, but that you wish to keep connected. If a colon is a 'suspender', a semicolon is more of a 'continuer'. Like a colon, a semicolon tells your reader that what you have said so far in a sentence is not all that you want to say. A colon, however, means that you are heading for closure; a semicolon, on the other hand, can be used to keep a sentence going. It would be rare to find a sentence with more than one colon in it, but you can stretch a sentence out with any number of semicolons, if you are so inclined.

The semicolon in 'balanced' sentences

The basic use of the semicolon can be shown most easily in balanced sentences, that is to say, in sentences where the two halves are similar in shape or wording and in which you could easily insert the phrase *on the other hand* in the part that follows the semicolon:

> *A colon means that you are heading for closure; a semicolon keeps things going.*

> *Dogs have masters and mistresses; cats have custodians.*

> *Once this house was surrounded by fields; now it is in the middle of a concrete jungle.*

In all these examples, both clauses – the one before and the one after the semicolon – are main clauses that could exist as complete sentences. *A semicolon keeps things going* is a perfectly adequate sentence. This, of course is another difference between the colon and the semicolon: the words that follow a colon need not form a complete sentence (although they often do).

If both halves of these sentences are complete in themselves and worthy to stand as independent sentences, it follows that they could be separated by a full stop.

> *Dogs have masters and mistresses. Cats have custodians.*

You may very well then ask why, if you can use a full stop, you should bother with a semicolon. The answer is that, in the kind of case we are discussing, you use the semicolon to show that you regard the two statements you are making not as two separate ideas, but as one idea that has two parts. Making a comparison or pointing out a contrast between cats and dogs is key to the particular idea that is being expressed. It is clearer to the reader that this is what you have in mind if you use a semicolon rather than a full stop.

The replaceability of semicolons

You can replace a semicolon with a full stop; you can also replace it with a comma and a linking word such as *and, but, while, whereas, although*, etc.

> *Dogs have masters and mistresses, but cats have custodians.*

Once this house was surrounded by fields, and now it is in the middle of a concrete jungle.

A colon means that you are heading for closure, while a semicolon keeps things going.

You should NOT use a semicolon in front of one of these linking words.

Most people appreciate really fine wines; but most fine wines are beyond ordinary people's pockets.

is incorrect. The correct punctuation mark here is a comma:

Most people appreciate really fine wines, but most fine wines are beyond ordinary people's pockets.

You can, however, use a semicolon in front of or together with a word such as *however, nevertheless, nonetheless, thus, consequently, hence* and *therefore* that expresses the idea of 'on the other hand' or 'because of this':

Most people appreciate really fine wines; however, most fine wines are beyond ordinary people's pockets.

I don't usually allow people to borrow my books; nevertheless, I might make an exception in your case.

He was notorious for his lack of conversation; consequently, he was seldom invited to dinner parties.

Again you may well ask: 'Why bother with a semicolon if it is not only replaceable by more "everyday" punctuation marks, but comes with irritating rules attached?' It is perfectly possible to write correctly and stylishly without ever sullying your paper with a semicolon. But if you want to use punctuation and language to the full, if you don't think longer sentences are necessarily a bad thing, and if you are apt to get fed up with using *and* and *but*, then it is worthwhile learning to use the semicolon and exploiting the particular possibilities of conveying meaning that it provides.

Let us try to make good this point by means of more examples:

> *Peter was wearing a bright yellow waistcoat and a pair of red trousers. Doreen was clad from head to foot in black.*

Here we have two sentences expressing two separate ideas. Without any additional context, we have no idea whether what Peter was wearing had any connection with what Doreen was wearing. The writer might be offering an overview of what everyone was wearing at a particular gathering:

> *Peter was wearing a bright yellow waistcoat and a pair of red trousers. Doreen was clad from head to foot in black. Jane wore the same brown frock she had worn the night before. Archibald was naked except for a loincloth.*

But if we want to suggest that there was more to it, that Peter's brightness and Doreen's sombreness were part of the same picture, that their clothes were a sign of their states of mind and that the one was colourful perhaps because the other rejected colour, or vice versa, then we have to put the two statements together in one sentence. We could link them with *and* or *but*, but this is a case where punctuation has the effect of 'less being more'.

> *Peter was wearing a bright yellow waistcoat and a pair of red trousers; Doreen was clad from head to foot in black.*

The distinction is slight and subtle, but the semicolon seems to create more of a sense of there being an 'atmosphere' between Peter and Doreen than:

> *Peter was wearing a bright yellow waistcoat and a pair of red trousers, but Doreen was clad from head to foot in black.*

Consider the following pairs of examples in the same light:

> *I took a quick glance in the mirror, and everything had changed since yesterday except me.*
>
> *I took a quick glance in the mirror; everything had changed since yesterday except me.*
>
> *Work gives meaning to our existence. I do so love work.*
>
> *Work gives meaning to our existence; I do so love work.*

I hope that you can detect a difference, but, in case you cannot, let us swiftly move on to firmer ground.

The semicolon and keeping the sentence going

We have so far been worrying away at sentences that do not stray very far from the balanced, two-part pattern. As was said at the beginning of this chapter, however, you are not restricted to using a single semicolon in any one sentence. If you have more than two statements that together make up a basic idea, you can, provided that each statement could form a complete sentence, link them all by means of semicolons. This is especially useful when you have a series of related things to report or describe:

> *Tim was idle; Tim never cleared up after himself; Tim broke things; Tim couldn't be trusted; Tim had no idea about money; Tim had no idea about anything. In short, nobody had a good word to say about poor old Tim.*

The first sentence is all about Tim. Chopping it up into six separate sentences would interrupt the flow and not give quite the same sense of a chorus of disapproval. Using commas here is strictly incorrect and, you might feel, allows the separate clauses to run together too much. The semicolon creates just the right balance between continuity and distinctness.

You can also use semicolons simply to stretch out a thought and a sentence:

> *Gill was in absolutely no mood to go to bed just yet; the night was young, as far as she was concerned; let the old, the boring and the faint-hearted retire to rest; with her energy levels undiminished and no commitments for the following morning, she was all for going on and on and on.*

The semicolon in lists

This topic has already been referred to in the chapter on the colon. While the items in most lists can be separated by commas, where the items are long, or contain commas themselves, it is preferable to divide them by semicolons. This demarcates the separate items much more clearly:

> *I looked at the list of resolutions I had made on the previous 1st of January and noted that I had resolved not to smoke, at least not before 6 p.m. on any particular day; not to get into debt, unless, of course, there was no other way of getting anything I wanted; not to overeat, overdrink, overbear, or overdo it; and not to bear false witness against my neighbour – though which neighbour my hastily scrawled note forgot to mention.*

Reprinting this sentence with commas substituted for the semicolons makes it clear why the semicolons are needed:

> *I looked at the list of resolutions I had made on the previous 1st of January and noted that I had resolved not to smoke, at least not before 6 p.m. on any particular day, not to get into debt, unless, of course, there was no other way of getting anything I wanted, not to overeat, overdrink, overbear, or overdo it, and not to bear false witness against my neighbour – though which neighbour my hastily scrawled note forgot to mention.*

Recap

- A semicolon allows a sentence to contain two or more separate statements that you want to combine as a single thought.

- The words that come before a semicolon and those that come - after it should both be capable of standing as a separate sentence.

- A semicolon should not be followed by *and* or *but*, but may be followed by linking words such as *however* and *nevertheless*.

- Semicolons should be used to separate longer and more complicated items in lists.

Exercise

Put a semicolon in the correct position in the following sentences (and add any other necessary punctuation):

1) *I came I saw I conquered.*

2) *Tuesday is when I usually go shopping Wednesday is when I visit friends.*

3) *They rejected the ultimatum out of hand thus war became inevitable.*

4) *There are several things you could say that you are busy that evening that you can't afford the restaurants they usually go to that there's a football match that you've promised your sister you'd watch with her or quite simply and truthfully that you don't want to go.*

Colon or semicolon?

Deciding whether a colon or semicolon is the correct punctuation mark to use is sometimes a matter of fine judgement. The grammatical distinction is quite straightforward:

- A colon can be followed by words that do not form a complete sentence; a semicolon cannot.

But, since a colon can also be followed by words that could otherwise stand alone as a sentence, you need to bear in mind the following distinction as well:

- A colon usually ushers in an explanation of the first part of the sentence, usually has the sense of *they are* or *that is to say (that)*, and tends towards closure; a semicolon does not offer an explanation, but simply suggests that what follows it is related to what precedes it, allows the sentence to continue and can be used several times in the same sentence.

Exercise

Decide whether the following sentences need a semicolon or a colon and insert one or the other in the correct position:

5) *There was one thing and one thing only that he wanted true love.*

6) *My brother owns a house in London my sister rents a flat in Barrow-in-Furness.*

7) *I would help you if I could it's just that I'm a little busy at the moment.*

8) *It's not the only invitation I've had in fact I'm invited out so often I rarely get an evening at home.*

9) *I've had invitations from the following people Jane, Sara, Jade and, last but not least, Antonia.*

10) *The weather was truly awful for the time of the year rain followed fog followed thunder followed hail.*

Brackets (( ), [ ], { }, < >)

The basics

Brackets come in several kinds (round, square, curly and angled). In ordinary writing (that is, outside mathematics), only round and square brackets are commonly used and their main function is to mark off material that is an addition to the sentence as a whole and generally incidental to it. They are also known as 'parentheses'.

Round brackets are the commonest kind – and when I use the word 'brackets' I shall be referring to them. Most of this section deals with their use, but square brackets have an additional function that merits special discussion.

What sort of material goes inside brackets?

Like the material that appears between a pair of commas, material that is placed inside brackets can always be removed from a sentence without affecting its basic meaning or making it incomplete. The material is usually of one of the following kinds:

- material that explains, clarifies or helps to identify something or someone mentioned in the main sentence:

  You should sauté the meat (fry it quickly in a little oil) before you add it to the stew.

  We made a special trip to Burano (one of the islands in the Venetian lagoon) to buy lace.

  Ms Robson (chair of the Ways and Means Committee) was asked to prepare a report.

- material that gives additional information, such as a person's dates or the Latin name of an animal of plant:

  Sir Francis Bacon (1561–1626) has often been credited with the authorship of the plays usually attributed to William Shakespeare.

  *The bluetit (*Pareus caeruleus*) is one of our commonest garden birds.*

(NB: if this sentence were printed in ordinary Roman type, the bluetit's Latin name would be in italics. The convention is that, when a sentence is printed in italic, words that would normally be italicised appear in Roman.)

- a personal comment by the writer about someone or something mentioned in the sentence:

  Garth (whom I was actually quite fond of) was being particularly obnoxious on that day.

  The replies given by the minister were (aren't they always?) very cautiously worded.

- words that specify who or what you mean or give examples of the kind of thing you mean:

  The permanent members of the United Nations Security Council (the USA, Russia, China, Britain and France) are all opposed to the plan.

> *Broadleaved trees, whether deciduous (like the oak and beech) or evergreen (like the holly), are far more susceptible to this disease.*

- the full form of an abbreviation following the abbreviation itself and explaining it, or an abbreviated form following the full form, especially when you are going to use the abbreviated form in the remainder of the text:

> *The DfID (Department for International Development) is sending representatives to the region.*

> *The Department for International Development (DfID) is sending representatives to the region.*

- a translation of a foreign word or title or an equivalent of a measurement or value:

> *A screening of Jean Renoir's La Règle du Jeu (The Rules of the Game) will be one of the highlights of the festival.*

> *The speed limit on ordinary French roads is 90 kph (56 mph).*

- a reference to another part of your text or to another text altogether (especially in an academic work):

> *The actual statistics (see Figure 1, below) are very revealing.*

Sir, Gerald Wainscott's recent article ('Roughhouse in Roehampton?', Enquirer 12/2/07) is a wanton slur on a well-respected institution.

This 'localization of globalization' (Merk and Tempest, 2006: 12) is a phenomenon that has already been extensively commented on in the literature (see, for example, Cooke, 1999; Frye, 2002).

Brackets and other punctuation

The material that you place inside brackets should be punctuated in the same way as it would be if the brackets were not there. The only exception to this rule is that you should not put a full stop inside brackets within a sentence, even if the bracketed material makes up a complete sentence (nor should you begin a complete sentence with a capital letter):

Michael returned to his mother's house (having, as he thought, nowhere else to go) to await developments.

He smashed his fist down on the bonnet of the car (the dent is still there) and swore violently.

You can, however, put a question mark or an exclamation mark at the end of bracketed material:

She liked (don't we all?) to look her best on such occasions.

> *He decided (God knows why!) to take the Christmas*
> *pudding out of the tin and boil it up in a kettle.*

The presence of bracketed material does not affect the punctuation of the main sentence. A closing bracket may be followed by a comma, colon, or semicolon. If the bracketed material comes at the end of the sentence, the full stop comes after the closing bracket.

> *We still haven't decided where to go for our holidays*
> *this year (but I rather fancy Norway).*

The only occasion on which a full stop should appear inside brackets is when the bracketed material is placed outside any other sentence. (In such instances the material can also begin with a capital letter.)

> *We still haven't decided where to go for our holidays*
> *this year. (Norway would be my destination of choice.)*

Brackets within brackets

It is possible to place an inner pair of brackets within an outer pair, but it is best to try to avoid a situation where two opening or closing brackets appear together:

> *The annual battle over where to go for our holidays is*
> *now on (my choice (Norway) does not appeal much to*
> *Mary).*

but preferably not:

> *The annual battle over where to go for our holidays is now on (my choice (Norway) is, as usual, at odds with Mary's (South Africa)).*

There are usually ways in which such a sentence can be rephrased or repunctuated to avoid such a clash:

> *The annual battle over where to go for our holidays is now on – my choice (Norway) is, as usual, at odds with Mary's (South Africa).*

It is possible to use square brackets inside round brackets. However, to avoid any confusion, it is best not to do this if you are using square brackets for the purpose outlined in the section below.

A single bracket

Brackets come in pairs. The only occasion on which you can use a single bracket is if you are labelling items in a list and putting them on separate lines:

> *I want you to:*
>
> *a) write to the manager of Adams Ltd*
> *b) file the reports I put on your desk last night*
> *c) reply to any outstanding e-mails*

If you include the labelled items in a sentence rather than listing them on separate lines, it is better to put the letters or numbers inside pairs of brackets:

> *There are three alternatives: (a) everybody uses their*
> *own car; (b) we share cars; (c) we hire a coach for the*
> *whole party.*

On a rather different note, you should avoid a situation where a single opening bracket appears at the end of a line or a single closing bracket appears at the beginning of a line:

> *In fact, she still hasn't given me an explanation (*
> *not that I really have the right to expect one) for why*
> *she left so early.*

Always make sure that at least one word accompanies a bracket at the end or beginning of a line.

Square brackets

The main use of square brackets is to mark changes that you make to quoted material or anything that you insert into quoted material.

Let us assume that someone has written or said, 'My main aim in life has been to secure the advancement of my people'. You may want to alter the sentence slightly to make it fit into your own sentence. In that case you put square brackets around the word or words that you have altered:

> *This does not really square with her claim that her*
> *'main aim in life has been to secure the advancement of*
> *[her] people'.*

Likewise, if you add an explanation or comment:

> *As one Eastwood resident remembers, 'We always knew young Bert [D H Lawrence] would never end up working down the pit.'*

It is also standard practice to put square brackets around the Latin word *sic*, which is used to indicate that a spelling mistake or some other error in a text you quote was in the original and not introduced by you:

> *According to the book, 'Gladiolae [sic] make a very acceptable thank-you present for your hostess.'*

Recap

- Brackets are used in pairs, except when you are labelling lists. Do not forget to put in the closing bracket.

- Round brackets are used to mark off material (such as an explanation or incidental comment) that is additional to the main sentence.

- Punctuation that belongs with this additional material goes inside the brackets.

- You should not put a full stop at the end of material inside brackets when the brackets are enclosed within a sentence.

- Square brackets are used for indicating changes or additions to quotations.

Exercise

Put round brackets in the appropriate places in the following sentences (and add any additional punctuation):

1) *Benvenuto Cellini 1500–1571 was a famous Italian goldsmith.*

2) *The local speciality is* bouillabaisse *a kind of fish soup or stew.*

3) *It has been suggested but not by me that we should walk the whole way.*

4) *Only three teams Arsenal, Liverpool and Manchester City now have any realistic chance of taking the final European place.*

5) *When you arrive don't be late come straight through to the back garden.*

The dash (-)

The basics

Try not to confuse a dash with a hyphen – a dash is longer. For the most part too, dashes separate, whereas hyphens join. If your word-processing skills are rudimentary, you may use a hyphen with a space at either end in place of a dash. It is better, however, to learn how to create a dash – on my PC, holding down Ctrl and pressing the hyphen key in the top right-hand corner of the keyboard above Enter does the trick, but you might have to experiment with yours.

Dashes frequently come in pairs, like brackets and commas, and do similar work. A single dash is used at the end of a sentence to separate off a comment that is generally emphatic and presents a contrast to what has gone before. Dashes are also used to do some linking, for instance in what are called 'number spans' (two figures that indicate the beginning and end of something, such as the first and last page of a particular section of a book).

The dash seems to be many people's punctuation mark of choice. A dash is much more conspicuous than a comma or a full stop and can – at least at a pinch – be used instead of a colon or semicolon. However, if all punctuation marks, apart from perhaps the full stop, were replaceable by dashes, there would be little point in this book. After dealing with one small typographical matter, we shall look at the entirely legitimate and well-established uses of the dash.

Em and en dashes

As far as printers, typesetters and keyboarders are concerned, dashes come in two sizes. The so-called em dash (or em rule) looks like this —; an en dash (or en rule) is somewhat shorter and looks like this –. Em dashes are normally used 'unspaced' (that is, without a space before and after them). En dashes are usually used 'spaced' (with spaces before and after) when they are used in ordinary text. En dashes, not em dashes, are used for linking work, and when acting as linkers they are normally used unspaced.

Pairs of dashes

The previous chapters on the comma and brackets should have familiarised you with the notion of material that is 'additional' to the main sentence. Material of that kind may also be separated off by a pair of dashes:

> *Then all four of them – Mildred, Annie, Christine and Jemima, not to mention the dog, of course – decided to strip off and go for a swim in the lake!*

> *When we get there – if we get there – I'll have something to say to him about his confounded map.*

> *The meal they offered us – smoked salmon, followed by soup, followed by roast beef and Yorkshire pudding, followed by spotted dick, followed by cheese, and all in enormous quantities – gave a whole new meaning to the phrase 'five a day'.*

Because the dash is a conspicuous punctuation mark, a pair of dashes is particularly useful for containing a fairly lengthy and quite complex addition. There are so many commas in the 'additional material' of the third sentence that using another pair of commas to fence it all in would not work. Also, in my view at least, dashes, in pairs or singly, seem most at home in writing that is vigorous if not slightly racy.

A single dash before a final comment

The dash has long been used at the end of sentences before a final emphatic comment that is slightly detached from the rest of the sentence, often because it stands to some degree in contrast to it:

> *Arthur did not answer, did not move, did not so much as bat an eyelid, but lay quietly in his bed – with a large kitchen knife protruding from his chest.*

> *She just has to make one phone call and your name will be all over the papers – not that I think for a moment that that's what she has in mind.*

A dash showing an interruption

One of the other uses of the dash is to show that a word or sentence is suddenly broken off before it can be completed:

> *'The girl over there, she's –' He broke off suddenly and dashed out of the room.*

Compare this use with that of the ellipsis (see the next chapter), which generally indicates that someone's voice or a sentence dies away.

The dash as linker

In number spans

The dash, specifically the en dash, is used, as mentioned earlier, in number spans:

> *The reign of Queen Victoria (1838–1901) is the longest to date of any British monarch.*

> *Pages 35–37 contain a detailed discussion of this point.*

An important thing to note is that when you use a dash in this way, you should not use prepositions such as *from, to* and *between*.

> *The compound contains 10–14 per cent potassium.*

> NOT
> *The compound contains from (or between) 10–14 per cent potassium.*

though you can, of course, write:

> *The compound contains from 10 to 14 (or between 10 and 14) per cent potassium.*

The dash is also used to give scores:

> *Wales beat France 45–21.*

Before nouns

An en dash is also the correct punctuation mark to use to link pairs of words before a noun in sentences like the following:

> *We shall be paying special attention to the parent–child relationship.*

The Murray–Federer match is bound to attract a large crowd.

Bristol–Barcelona flights are subject to long delays.

It is important to distinguish between linkages of this type and ordinary linkages with a hyphen (see the chapter on THE HYPHEN). You can usually change this type of combination into a phrase using the word *between* (the relationship between parent and child; the match between Murray and Federer). It almost always involves two (or occasionally more) distinct categories of things or people, or two named places, countries, people or organisations who are, so to speak, partners in something. The range of words that can be linked with a hyphen and placed before a noun is much wider:

a two-day event (hyphen)

a three-party coalition (hyphen)

a Labour–Liberal Democrat coalition (dash)

Recap

- A dash is considerably longer than a hyphen.

- The dash is a conspicuous and fairly dramatic punctuation mark.

- Dashes are used in pairs to separate off an often fairly complex addition inside the sentence.

- A single dash separates off an emphatic comment at the end of a sentence.

- En dashes are used in number spans and to link two words, which represent 'partners' in a relation of some kind, before a noun.

Exercise

Insert a dash or dashes in the appropriate places in these sentences:

1) *I didn't read it all I simply didn't have enough time but the bit that I did read was very good.*

2) *They're going to build a new kitchen and conservatory on at the back and landscape the whole garden if they can find the money, that is.*

3) *The events of the years 1648 1653 had a profound effect on the young king Louis XIV.*

4) *There was no reason at least none that Helen was aware of why they should not be married at once.*

The ellipsis (. . .)

The basics

An ellipsis (also called an 'omission mark' or a 'suspension [mark]') consists of a row of three dots or full stops and does . . . well, it essentially does exactly what its alternative names suggest: it indicates that something has been left out of a sentence or a quotation, or that a sentence is left unfinished. The number of dots in an ellipsis is fixed at three – no more, no less. If you encounter a row of four dots, then you should assume that the first or last of those dots is intended to be understood as a full stop.

The ellipsis in quotations

It often happens that you do not wish, or do not need, to quote the whole of a particular passage in order to illustrate or support a point you are making. When you omit a word, phrase or sentence from the original material, you should indicate the fact to your reader by replacing the words you have missed out with an ellipsis.

Suppose that from the following passage you only wish to quote the words that have been underlined:

> In the next sonnet in the sequence, <u>Shakespeare</u>, after first asking whether he should compare the addressee to a summer's day, immediately <u>rejects the comparison</u> and spends four lines <u>describing ways in which summer days can be unlovely and intemperate</u> and are subject to unpredictable change.

You should show that you have shortened the passage by writing it down as follows:

> *Far from likening the young man to a summer's day, 'Shakespeare . . . rejects the comparison . . . describing ways in which summer days can be unlovely and intemperate.'*

You will note that there are no ellipses at the start and end of the quotation, even though the opening and closing phrases in the original have been left out. Readers understand that quotations are selected in the main from longer passages. Generally speaking, you can begin at the first word that you need and end at the last word you need without ellipses before and after. Only put them in if you wish to call special attention to the fact that things were said before and after that you have not quoted:

> *He was speaking to someone as I passed by, and I overheard the words '. . . definitely gone for good, but . . .'. Who or what he was speaking of, however, I have no idea.*

Using an ellipsis to end a sentence or indicate a pause

An ellipsis is often used to indicate that there is a pause in a sentence or that a sentence is left unfinished, either because the speaker could not find the proper words or ran out of them or because he or she did not need to say any more since the intended meaning was already clear:

> *'I want . . . that is to say, I'm trying . . . or, at least, I would . . . if I could . . .'*

'I'm sorry, I just . . .' His voice tailed away, and he ended with a helpless shrug.

'No more funny business, or else . . .' He drew his finger once across his throat.

The ellipsis tends to suggest that a person's voice dies away or that he or she deliberately leaves something unsaid. To indicate that someone is abruptly cut off, it is usually better to use a dash:

'I ought to remind you that the penalty for –' 'I know all about the penalties,' I interrupted.

The use of the ellipsis at the end of a sentence is not confined to dialogue.

Her voice droned on and on . . . I woke up with a start to find her standing over me with a malicious gleam in her eye.

There would be other days and better days. Oh yes, those other better days would certainly come . . .

In the first example, the ellipsis creates a pause and aptly suggests the woman continuing to drone, the speaker nodding off and the passage of time that elapses before he or she is rudely awakened. In the second, readers are invited to continue the thought or the story in almost any way they choose and, since this involves looking ahead, it seems more appropriate to leave things open by using an ellipsis than to bring them to a definite close by using a full stop.

The ellipsis and other punctuation marks

One of the purposes of the ellipsis is to indicate that a sentence is incomplete or that the action or state described in the sentence continues. It is not usually necessary, therefore, nor would it be altogether logical, to add a full stop. The following sentence should, however, begin with a capital letter.

If, for any reason, you do need a full stop before or after an ellipsis, you should try to indicate that it is a separate punctuation mark by leaving an extra space:

> *'Blessed are the meek . . . .' Is the reason Our Lord goes on to give for saying that the meek are blessed not a very strange and unexpected one?*

Other punctuation marks can follow an ellipsis in the normal way:

> *'Can we . . . ?' She gestured towards the door.*
>
> *'What the . . . !'*

Recap

- An ellipsis consists of a row of three dots or full stops.

- It is used to indicate that a word or words have been omitted from a quotation.

- It is also used to indicate a pause or leave a sentence unfinished.

- An ellipsis may be followed by another punctuation mark. A full stop after an ellipsis is a separate mark, however, not simply a fourth dot in the row.

The slash (/)

The basics

The best way of describing the slash is to say that it is a simple and/or relatively informal way of presenting alternatives. It is also used in some abbreviations, in presenting dates and as a substitute for the dash in one of its linking roles.

Presenting alternatives

If you put two (or more) words together and separate them by a slash, the reader assumes that the words are alternatives and that one or the other of them will apply:

> *He/she should have previous experience of retail management.*

> *You should bring some form of identification (passport/birth certificate/driving licence).*

> *The owner/tenant is responsible for the section of the back lane bordering his/her property.*

Other uses of the slash

The slash is used in some abbreviations:

> *a/c* (account)

> *c/o* (care of)

It is also used in dates to indicate a period of time that runs from one year into the next:

the 2007/8 tax year

during the 1979/80 season

It can also be used in place of an en dash when 'partnered' names are placed in front of a noun:

They're showing the Brunson/Lawley fight on TV tonight.

We took the Brussels/Cologne/Basel route to avoid paying tolls on French motorways.

Finally, and in a completely different context, the slash is used to mark the divisions between lines of poetry when you do not write them out one below the other:

'I wandered lonely as a cloud / That floats on high o'er dales and hills . . .'

'Come into the garden, Maud, / For the black bat, night, has flown, / Come into the garden, Maud, / I am here at the gate alone.'

Recap

- The slash is principally used for presenting alternatives of the he/she kind.

- It is used in showing periods of time that run from one year into the next.

- It may be used in place of an en dash between words in front of a noun.

- It is used to show divisions between lines of poetry that are not shown one below the other.

Quotation marks ('', " ")

The basics

The main purpose of quotation marks (also known as 'quotes' and 'inverted commas') is to show that something you have written down was first spoken or written by somebody else. They are also used to pick out and highlight particular words or phrases in a sentence.

Single or double quotation marks

Computer and typewriter keyboards give you the option of using single quotes (' ') or double quotes (" ").

General British practice is to use single quotation marks for most purposes and only to use double quotation marks for quoted or highlighted words that fall inside a quotation:

> *'I've got the whole of "To be or not to be" off by heart already,' said Rufus.*

> *'I don't know what you mean by "wishy-washy"', I said, 'but that certainly doesn't sound like my Harry.'*

As you can see from the second example, it is perfectly permissible to have three quotation marks in a row under certain circumstances.

General American practice is the exact opposite of the British. American writers use double quotation marks for most purposes with single quotation marks inside them.

Whichever system you choose, you should stick to it. Well-intentioned people sometimes use double quotes for reporting speech or quoting from books and single quotation marks to high-light particular words. This is unnecessary and may, indeed, cause the very confusion it is seeking to avoid.

Quotation marks and quoting

You should only use quotation marks to enclose the exact words used by someone else in speech or writing. In particular, you should not use quotation marks around indirect speech:

> '*I'll meet you there at half past seven,*' *said Sheila.*

> *Sheila said that she would meet us there at half past seven.*

> NOT
> *Sheila said* '*that she would meet us there at half past seven*'.

Here are two more correct examples:

> *I really love the lines* '*If you can meet with triumph and disaster / And treat those two impostors just the same*'.
> (exact words – direct speech – in quotation marks)

but

> *My favourite lines are the ones about meeting triumph and disaster and treating them just the same.*
> (indirect speech – no quotation marks)

The golden rule, it will bear repeating once again, is only to use quotation marks around the exact words spoken or written by someone else. But you can, of course, break up those words and insert something in the middle:

> *'I'll meet you there,' whispered Sheila, 'at half past seven.'*

> *Most of us can expect to 'meet with triumph and disaster' in the course of a lifetime, but few of us, perhaps, will consider them 'impostors' or be able to treat them 'just the same'.*

(For the use of punctuation within quotation marks, see page 126.)

Quotation marks used to pick out words

Quotation marks are often used to show that a particular word, phrase or letter is being considered as a word, phrase or letter independently and does not contribute to the meaning of the sentence in the normal way:

> *'Gas' is a three-letter word.*

> *Do you spell your name with 'ph' or a 'v'?*

> *The phrase 'primus inter pares' means 'first among equals'.*

You should, as the final example shows, also put the definition between inverted commas when you explain the meaning of something.

There is an alternative method of picking out words for this purpose, which is to put them into italics. That is the method generally used in this book.

You can also, as a writer, use quotation marks to call attention to words that you think are particularly unusual or that are outside their normal context or your normal vocabulary. Publishers and printers call these 'scare quotes'. The words in question tend to be examples of technical jargon, slang or dialect, or clichés or euphemisms.

> *He's what the police often refer to as 'an ordinary decent criminal'.*

> *A 'top down' structuring of local action is more prevalent in Europe.*

> *He seemed to be especially pleased with that goal because he 'nutmegged' the goalkeeper.*

> *He was annoyed because he'd got some grease from the 'barbie' on his 'strides'.*

> *Does a 'refuse disposal operative' do anything else besides emptying dustbins?*

There is a sense in all these examples that writers are using other people's words, even if they are not quoting a particular person directly.

Quotation marks in titles

It is general practice in *handwritten* texts to put the titles of books, plays, films, operas and similar works in inverted commas:

> *We went to see 'Hamlet' at the National Theatre.*

> *When you've finished 'Eats, Shoots and Leaves', can I*
> *borrow it?*

Be careful not to put the name of a character into inverted commas if it happens to be the same as that of the work:

> *He played Hamlet until he was fifty and then moved on*
> *to King Lear.*

but

> *She directed 'Hamlet' last year, and this year she's*
> *directing 'King Lear'.*

> *His article 'Four theses in the study of China's urbaniza-*
> *tion' was published in the* International Journal of
> Urban and Regional Research *last year.*

When you have italics available, however, it is better to put titles in italics rather than inverted commas.

In academic works it is often the practice to put the titles of shorter or minor works, for example journal articles, short stories or individual poems, into inverted commas while the names of the journals or collections in which they appear are given in italics:

(Note that in this instance, for clarity, I have reversed my normal use of italics for examples.)

Punctuation in quotations

Remarks on the use of various punctuation marks in quotations are given in the relevant chapters. This is, however, a good opportunity to draw all that material together and to present a few general rules.

Putting punctuation inside or outside the quotation marks

The general rules are these:

- Punctuation that belongs with the material that you are quoting goes inside the quotation marks.

- Punctuation that belongs to the sentence in which the quotation appears goes outside the quotation marks.

- If words you quote at the end of a sentence end with a question mark or exclamation mark, there is no need to add an additional full stop to close the main sentence. You may, however, add an additional question mark or exclamation mark outside the final quotation mark if the main sentence needs one.

- If words you quote at the end of a sentence do not themselves form a complete sentence, the full stop belongs to the main sentence and goes outside the quotation marks.

Let me illustrate these rules with some examples:

> *They immediately started shouting, 'Help! Police!'*

The exclamation marks belong with the words that were shouted; they go inside the quotation marks. There is no need to place an additional full stop after the closing quotation mark.

> *Who was it who shouted 'Help! Police!'?*

In this case the exclamation marks remain inside the quotation marks, but the main sentence is constructed as a question. An additional question mark is needed, and it goes outside the quotation marks.

> *I got no answer when I shouted, 'Who goes there?'*

In this example, on the other hand, the question mark belongs with the challenge and goes inside the quotation marks. As in the first of these examples, there is no need to add an additional full stop.

> *When you ask 'Who goes there?', what do people usually reply?*

The first question mark here belongs with the sentry's challenge; it goes inside the quotation marks. The comma belongs to the surrounding sentence and links the subordinate clause containing the quotation to the main clause; it remains outside the quotation marks.

> *Why did she not answer when you shouted, 'Who goes there?'?*

This is one of the rare occasions when the same punctuation mark is repeated. There is no need, remember, to add an additional full stop when a quotation ends with an exclamation mark or a question mark, but you should add an additional question mark or exclamation mark if the main sentence requires one.

> *What I actually said was, 'I left the key in the top drawer of my desk.'*

Here the words quoted form a full sentence; the full stop therefore belongs with them and falls inside the quotation marks.

> *When I asked him where the key was, he said 'in the top*
> *drawer of my desk'.*

Here the words quoted do not form a full sentence; the full stop closes the main sentence and goes outside the quotation marks. As it does in this final example:

> *It's all about being able to 'keep your head when all*
> *about you are losing theirs'.*

Beginning quotations with capital letters

The general rules are:

- When the words that you quote form a complete sentence they begin with a capital letter, no matter where they come in the surrounding sentence.

- If the words you quote do not form a complete sentence, they start with a small letter, unless they are placed at the beginning of the surrounding sentence.

Here are some examples:

> *I asked her whether I could take one, and she said, 'Be*
> *my guest.'*

The quoted words form a complete sentence; they begin with a capital letter. That complete sentence ends with a full stop; it belongs inside the quotation marks.

> *If I hear him say 'custard tart' in that sneering voice one*
> *more time, I shall hit him!*

The quoted words are not a full sentence; they begin with a small letter.

> *'When I was young . . .' seems to be her favourite way of starting a sentence.*

Although they do not constitute a full sentence, the quoted words come at the beginning of the surrounding sentence and so begin with a capital letter.

For more examples, look back to the previous section.

Punctuation with reporting verbs, especially in the middle of quotations

Let me just remind you that a 'reporting verb' is a verb such as *say*, *remark*, *comment*, *whisper* or *wonder* that is used to cue in a quotation or a piece of indirect speech. Here are the general rules for using punctuation with these verbs:

- The rule that punctuation belonging with the words you quote goes inside the quotation marks, while punctuation belonging to the main sentence goes outside them, still applies.

- If the words you quote before a reporting verb form a full sentence, you should replace the full stop with a comma, which goes inside the quotation marks. You should not, however, replace either a question mark or an exclamation mark with a comma.

- When a reporting verb and its subject (*she said*, etc) interrupt a quotation, they are enclosed in a pair of commas.

- If the words you quote before a reporting verb do not form a full sentence, logically the comma should go outside the quotation marks, but many people do not follow this logic.

- It is usual to put a comma after a reporting verb before you begin a quotation. In some rare instances, you can replace the comma with a colon.

Again, here are some examples to illustrate these rules:

> *'That is a very difficult question to answer,' said Saskia.*

What Saskia said formed a full sentence. The original full stop is replaced with a comma, which is placed within the quotation marks.

> *'Can't you ask me something easier?' complained Saskia.*

The original words were a question. Question marks and exclamation marks are not replaced by commas, but do remain within the quotation marks.

> *'That is a very difficult question to answer,' said Saskia, 'I shall need some time to think about it.'*

Saskia spoke two full sentences. The reporting verb and subject are enclosed by commas. The first goes inside the first pair of inverted commas, the second remains outside the second pair.

> *'That', said Saskia, 'is a very difficult question to answer.'*

The single word that precedes the reporting verb is obviously not a full sentence and there would be no comma at that point in her original sentence. Logically, the comma is simply there to bracket the reporting verb and should fall outside the quotation marks. (Despite the interruption, what Saskia said was a full sentence so the final full stop goes inside the quotation marks. The second part of her statement, however, not being a full sentence, begins with a small letter.)

However, many people feel that a comma placed outside the quotation marks, as in the previous example, seems detached or looks wrong. They therefore prefer to put it inside the quotation marks:

> 'That,' said Saskia, 'is a very difficult question to answer.'

This is another of those cases where you have to opt for one system or the other and stick to it.

> 'That, you know,' said Saskia, 'is a very difficult question to answer.'

In this case, the phrase *you know* would be enclosed in commas in the original statement. Punctuation that belongs with the words you quote remains inside the quotation marks. There is no need to add an additional comma, even though the words that come before the reporting verb still do not make up a full sentence.

> *I had become used to getting prompt and illuminating replies from Saskia, the brains of the department, and was, accordingly, rather disappointed by her reply: 'That is a very difficult question to answer and I shall need a long time to think about it.'*

You can introduce a quotation (usually a fairly long one) with a colon. The colon should then be performing its normal function, which is to introduce material that adds to explains or clarifies what has gone before. In this case, we could say, the nature of Saskia's reply explains the speaker's disappointment.

Recap

- Quotation marks may be single or double. British practice is to use single quotation marks with double quotation marks for quotes within quotes.

- You should only put quotation marks around the exact words spoken or written by somebody else.

- Indirect speech does not require quotation marks.

- Quotation marks can also be placed around single letters, words or phrases that you wish to consider as letters, words or phrases independent of the sentence in which they appear.

- You can also use quotation marks to pick out words that are not words that you or your reader would normally know or use.

- Punctuation that goes with the words you quote should be put inside quotation marks. Punctuation that goes with the main sentence should be put outside the quotation marks.

Exercises

Put quotation marks in the appropriate places in these sentences:

1) *Do you spell your name with a C or a K?*

2) *Let's get out of here, he whispered.*

3) *You should pronounce the word wind to rhyme with kind.*

4) *I shall be reciting a very famous poem that begins If you can keep your head . . . , he announced.*

5) *She said that it was a very difficult question to answer.*

6) *I know that he calls it a dooberry, but what do ordinary people call it?*

Put quotation marks and other punctuation into the following sentences:

7) *She said I'll go and call a cab*

8) *Have you got a pen I could borrow he enquired*

9) *That I remarked is something best left for the committee to decide*

10) *He keeps on calling out where did you put my car keys*

11) *My God exclaimed Celia you don't mean he actually asked you to marry him*

3 Punctuation Inside Words

The apostrophe (')

The basics

The apostrophe's basic function is to indicate that something has been missed out of a word or phrase. *Twelve o'clock* is a shortened form of the old-fashioned phrase 'twelve of the clock'; *don't* is a contraction of 'do not'; the word *fo'c'sle* (this is the usual spelling given in *The New Oxford Dictionary of English*; *fo'c's'le* also exists) is a briefer rendering of the nautical term 'forecastle'; and *the '60s* is a short way of referring to the 1960s or the equivalent decade of another century.

The commonest use of the apostrophe, however, is to indicate possession. Attached to the end of a name or noun, it indicates that the next thing mentioned belongs to the person or thing designated by the first name or noun: *Margaret's handkerchief; the car's engine; the cars' engines; our cat Mittens'(s) favourite hiding place.*

The commonest misuse of the apostrophe is to form the plurals of ordinary nouns. There are a number of extraordinary and usually very short words, however, which can correctly form their plural with an apostrophe: *There are four s's in 'Mississippi'.*

Let us now look at these three functions in turn.

The apostrophe indicating omission

Apart from *o'clock*, the commonest forms with letters taken out and replaced by apostrophes consist of:

- simple verbs plus *not*:

  can not – can't

  have not – haven't

  would not – wouldn't

  will not – won't

- personal pronouns (the words *I*, *you*, *he*, *she*, *it*, *we* and *they*) plus a shortening of one of the forms of *to be* or *to have* or of *will*, *shall*, *would* or *should*:

  I am – I'm

  you will – you'll

  we have – we've

  they would – they'd

- words such as *that*, *there*, *who* and *where* plus one of the same verb forms:

  There'll be trouble!

  Who'd have thought it?

Where's he gone?

These shortened forms are used all the time in spoken English and very frequently in the written variety. It is vital to remember that they must be spelt with an apostrophe, since several of them contain the same letters as ordinary words:

> *she'll – shell*
>
> *we'll – well*
>
> *he'll – hell*
>
> *won't – wont* (meaning 'habit', as in *as was his wont*)
>
> *can't – cant* (meaning 'insincere and sanctimonious talk')

The potential for confusion between the forms with and without apostrophe in real-life sentences is probably small. But – unless you are setting out to be a radical spelling reformer like George Bernard Shaw (who insisted on writing *I shant come*, etc.) – you will be thought either ignorant or slapdash by respectable readers if you leave the apostrophes out.

I should perhaps make one small style point. When speaking, we often tag contractions such as *'ve* and *'ll* onto the ends of ordinary nouns. But while it may be all right to say

> *The neighbours've been complaining.*

or

> *Another bus'll be along in a minute.*

neither looks good in writing. Unless you are deliberately trying to imitate informal speech, write the verb out in full:

The neighbours have been complaining.

Four cases of potential confusion

There are four particular cases in which it is all too easy to slip up and cause confusion by mistakenly putting in or leaving out an apostrophe.

The first involves the possessive pronouns *hers, ours, yours* and *theirs*. None of them is spelt with an apostrophe, but, because they indicate possession (and indicating possession is the apostrophe's commonest function), people often make the mistake of putting an apostrophe in. Try to remember that *mine*, the possessive pronoun that goes with *I*, does not end with an *s*, so no sensible person would think of putting an apostrophe into it. (Neither would anyone really want to put an apostrophe between the *i* and the *s* in *his*.) The other words are of exactly the same class and perform exactly the same function. They too have no apostrophe.

The book is mine.

The book is his.

The book is hers. (NOT *her's*)

Thine is the kingdom, the power and the glory.

Yours is the Earth and everything that's in it . . . (NOT *Your's*)

That particular piece of land isn't theirs, it's ours.
(NOT *their's* and *our's*)

The second case that causes confusion involves *your* and *you're*. Because they are pronounced the same way and the difference in spelling is slight, it only takes a second's inattention to write the one instead of the other (especially to write *your* when *you're* is correct):

You're late! (NOT *Your*)

You're pulling my leg! (NOT *Your*)

I haven't got a clue what you're talking about! (NOT *your*)

but

Your late father gave it to me. (NOT *You're*)

and, less obviously,

Your mentioning your late father reminded me of something he once said to me. (NOT *you're* in either case)

Most readers of this book will know perfectly well that *your* means 'belonging to you' and that *you're* is a contraction of 'you are'. The mistake is generally made not through ignorance, but through haste and inattention or a slip of the finger. The remedy is to inspect what you have written carefully, after you have written it. If you are in any real doubt as to which is the correct form, then try inserting *you are* into the sentence. If you put it into the final example above – which contains a somewhat uncommon use of the possessive adjective – you make nonsense of the sentence:

> *You are mentioning you are late father reminded*
> *me . . .*

The third danger area involves *who's* and *whose*, which, once again, are often inadvertently confused because of their similarity in sound and spelling and because they are both generally used in questions. The important thing to remember, of course, is that *who's* is a contraction of *who is* or *who has*:

> *Who's willing to volunteer?* (NOT *Whose*)
>
> *Who's got my socks?* (NOT *Whose*)
>
> *Guess who's coming to dinner.* (NOT *whose*)

while *whose* asks whom something belongs to:

> *Whose are those socks?* (NOT *Who's*)
>
> *Whose did you say they are?* (NOT *Who's*)
>
> *This pullover I'm holding is whose?* (NOT *who's*)
>
> *Guess whose autograph I managed to get.* (NOT *who's*)

Again, whoever you are and however good your spelling and grammar generally are, you too can make this mistake through inattention. Always be aware that this pitfall lies in wait; check your writing and, if in doubt, insert *who is* or *who has* into the sentence and see what happens.

The fourth and final stumbling block is the old favourite *it's* and *its*. With an apostrophe, it means 'it is' or 'it has'; without an apostrophe, it means 'belonging to it'. There is nothing really memorable and snappy to help engrave this in your memory. You simply have to recollect that none of the other small possessive words we use all the time has an apostrophe, not *his* and not *yours, ours, hers* and *theirs* (although the latter are not used in front of a noun), and neither does *its*. Likewise, being contractions, *he's* and *she's* do have apostrophes, and so, for the same reason, does *it's*.

> *Its top has worked loose.* (NOT *It's*)
>
> *The garden's not looking its best at the moment.* (NOT *it's*)
>
> *The poor little cat has hurt its paw.* (NOT *It's*)

but

> *It's top of the charts at the moment.* (NOT *Its*)
>
> *It's never been the same since Charles sat on it.* (NOT *Its*)
>
> *You can't go out because it's raining.* (NOT *its*)

and

> *It's lost its little thingy.* (NOT *Its lost it's little thingy*)

The apostrophe showing possession

There is no authentic way of linking the use of the apostrophe to shorten words and phrases with its use as an indication of what belongs to whom or what. But, if you wish to imagine ancient users of English becoming fed up with writing or saying *Robin Hood, his bow and arrow* and shortening it to *Robin Hood's bow and arrow*, you may, so long as you don't convince yourself that this is what actually happened. (You can put the fact that *Maid Marian, her embroidery basket*, became *Maid Marian's embroidery basket* down to the ingrained sexism of those ancient days.)

- When a noun is in the singular (that is, when it refers to only one person or thing), you show possession by adding *'s*:

    the cat's whiskers

    the bee's knees

    I don't give a monkey's.

- When two or more people own the same thing, you only need one apostrophe, which you attach to the last name in the list:

    Cheryl and John's house

    We're going round to Peter and Angela's tonight.

    Soo, Grabbit and Runne's legal ethics

(If you were to attach an apostrophe to more than one name, you would imply that the people do not share possession of something. *Henry's and Molly's children are learning to get along* suggests that both Henry and Molly have children from previous relationships who are in the process of becoming one big happy family.)

- When a noun is plural (that is, when it refers to more than one person or thing) and ends in *s*, you simply add an apostrophe:

  the parents' concerns

  my relatives' addresses

Needless to say, when the words are spoken, there is no discernible difference between *the cat's whiskers* and *the cats' whiskers*. Likewise, the difference in writing is only slight. Where you place the apostrophe, however, can make a considerable difference to the meaning:

  Our neighbour's fences have been blown down. (one neighbour, several fences)

  Our neighbours' fences have been blown down. (several neighbours and several fences)

- When a plural form ends in a letter other than *s*, you add *'s* as you would with a singular:

  the women's toilets

  the children's toys

  the media's appetite for sensation

- When a singular noun ends in *s*, you should generally follow the standard procedure and form the possessive by adding *'s*:

  the bus's tyres

the princess's wedding

Jess's progress at school

the hippopotamus's bad temper

It is, however, permissible, and sometimes conventional, to omit the additional *s* when forming the possessive of a name of two syllables or more:

It is conventional to write:

Jesus' teachings and Moses' leadership

instead of

Jesus's teachings and Moses's leadership

It is permissible to write:

Inspector Rebus' detective work

and

Mary Hopkins' hit record

It is altogether preferable to avoid a big buzzing sound at the end of a word and so to say or write:

Ulysses' homecoming

Socrates' method of arguing

Conventions aside, the best rule to follow is to write down what you would say – and to use your common sense. After all, a purist following the guidelines given above might write:

Mr Jones's car is bigger than Mr Hopkins'.

This is all very well on paper, but, because you could not say it without fear of misunderstanding, it is probably better to balance up the apostrophes and write:

Mr Jones's car is bigger than Mr Hopkins's.

The apostrophe and plurals

It would be helpful if we could simply issue a blanket statement to the effect that forming a plural with an apostrophe *s* is always wrong. So-called 'greengrocer's plurals'

potato's

lettuce's

have been derided often enough. Everyone seems to have seen a sign somewhere that contains a similar mistake. *Cream Tea's* is often cited. If you type the characters *apostrophe's* into an Internet search engine, you get a large number of hits. Many of the sites use the term tongue in cheek; many don't.

Please, please, do not introduce apostrophes into plurals where they are not needed.

They are not needed, for instance, in the plurals of abbreviations:

MPs (NOT *MP's*)

DVDs (NOT *DVD's*)

Nor are they needed when you add an *s* to figures:

the 1990s (NOT *the 1990's*)

Six 8s are 48.

It is, however, customary to use an apostrophe when adding *s* to a lower-case letter of the alphabet:

How many n's are there in 'millennium'?

Mind your p's and q's.

(Without an apostrophe, confusion could obviously arise over the plural of *a*, *i* and *u*, although

She got three straight As.

is perfectly acceptable.)

It is also customary to use an apostrophe with some short words:

Both our ex's were at the wedding.

Don't invite me to any more of these posh do's.

As a general rule, however, if you see an apostrophe in a word that is obviously intended as a plural, it is wrong.

Tricky issues

We usually speak, for convenience's sake, of the apostrophe as indicating possession. But there are many instances in which possession really has nothing to do with the matter in hand. The phrase I have just used, *for convenience's sake*, is a case in point. It is obvious that it is an alternative way of saying *for the sake of convenience*, just as *the boy's coat* is an alternative, and much neater, way of saying *the coat of the boy*. The latter example clearly has to do with possession, however, while the former does not. It is sometimes best to ignore the issue of possession when considering whether to use an apostrophe.

The *for . . . sake* construction is my first tricky issue. Whatever the meaning or function of the *'s*, it is obvious that there ought to be one in:

> *for heaven's sake*
>
> and
>
> *for pity's sake*

That is the way these phrases are always written, and always spoken if they are pronounced carefully. But we frequently say *for convenience sake* and *for goodness sake*; ought we to insert an apostrophe? The answer is strictly 'yes':

> *for convenience' sake* and *for goodness' sake*

but nowadays you have to be something of a purist to insist on these apostrophes. In these two cases, it is generally acceptable to leave the apostrophes out.

The second tricky issue concerns time; in particular, phrases such as *in ten years' time*. They ought to be written with an apostrophe, even though, once again, the idea of possession simply confuses the issue.

To grasp the logic, you have to start counting from one. If *in ten years time* were correct, then, logically, the equivalent for *one year* would be *in one year time* or *in a year time*. This is not what we say. We always say *in one year's* or *a year's time*. Following the same pattern, we should write *in ten years' time, in five months' time* etc. By the same token, *three months' imprisonment, four weeks' holiday* (just as we would say *a fortnight's holiday*) and *six weeks' waiting time* are correct, and to omit the apostrophe in any of them would be incorrect.

Notice that in all these cases the apostrophe comes after the *s* – *ten year's time* (which I have seen written) is completely incorrect. It is also important to bear in mind that the apostrophe is only needed in front of a noun such as *time, imprisonment,* etc. You do not need an apostrophe in phrases such as:

ten years later

six months ago

three months pregnant

and

five minutes late

The third tricky issue concerns lavatories. Most people would probably expect to have to put in an apostrophe when they write:

a ladies'/gents' lavatory

But should you retain the apostrophe if you write down such commonplace sayings as:

> *There's a ladies(') just down the corridor.*
>
> *Can you tell me the way to the gents(')?*

The answer depends on how dedicated you are to preserving the apostrophe. As with *for goodness(') sake*, strict grammar requires one, but as *a ladies* and *a gents* are now considered nouns in their own right, it is acceptable to leave the apostrophe out (especially if a capital letter is used: *the Ladies* and *the Gents*).

Recap

- An apostrophe indicates that a word or phrase is missing a letter or letters found in its full form.

- Apostrophes are always necessary in forms such as *aren't*, *I'll* and *there's*.

- An apostrophe indicates possession.

- Singular nouns add *'s* to form the possessive; plural nouns simply add the apostrophe.

- Singular nouns and names ending in *s* generally also add *'s* to form the possessive. In some cases, however, you need only add the apostrophe.

- Apart from lower-case letters and a few short nouns, no words, abbreviations or figures need an apostrophe to form their plural.

Exercise

Add apostrophes (or 's), where needed, to the following sentences:

1) *I cant see why hes making so much fuss.*

2) *Those suitcases arent yours, theyre ours.*

3) *Thats Peters book, isnt it?*

4) *The boys bikes have been left out in the rain.* (There are several boys.)

5) *Its got its head stuck between the railings.*

6) *I am now going to recite you one of Robert Burns most famous poems.*

7) *Wheres the Smiths house?*

8) *Freddy and Jean aunt gave it to them.*

The hyphen (-)

The basics

The basic, long-standing function of the hyphen is to link together two or more existing words, or word units, to form a new word. That has not changed.

What has changed, and changed drastically, is the frequency with which the hyphen is used. Once upon a time the hyphen was a well-established part of many common words. *To-day* and *to-morrow*, for instance, are listed as the only spellings of the words we know as *today* and *tomorrow* in a copy of *The Shorter Oxford English Dictionary* that I bought in the 1970s (although the Oxford University Press had not then properly revised that work since the late 1930s). But, whereas in the past people seem to have been happy to spell words with hyphens, nowadays they prefer to spell them either as one word (*teaspoon* not *tea-spoon*) or as two separate words (*tea caddy* not *tea-caddy*).

This might appear to have simplified matters, but it has not really done so. It is often difficult to decide whether to spell common compounds as single words or as two words. Dictionaries disagree. *The New Oxford English Dictionary* (1999) gives *egg cup*, *egghead* and *egg-nog*; *Collins English Dictionary* (2001) gives *egg cup*, *egghead* and *eggnog*; the *Bloomsbury English Dictionary* (2004) gives *eggcup*, *egghead* and *eggnog*. This seems to suggest that the present situation is fluid, but that there is a trend towards spelling as a single word. Fortunately, there is little chance of real confusion in meaning in such cases, but it would be nice to have firm ground to stand on when spelling.

What is clear is that the hyphen has departed for good and all from most words of this kind. That does not mean that the hyphen is never used in present-day English; it does mean that using too many hyphens will make your text look old-fashioned. Let us now look at situations where hyphens are still required.

Hyphenated words

Hyphens are still standard in words of the following types:

- two-word written forms of numbers between 20 and 100:

    forty-six

    seventy-nine

- words consisting of a combination of more than two other words:

    free-for-all

    jack-of-all-trades

    ne'er-do-well

    rough-and-tumble

    sister-in-law

- words made by attaching a prefix (a word unit such as *anti-*, *pro-* or *un-* attached to the front of another word) to a word beginning with a capital letter:

    anti-Christian

    pro-Marxist

un-American

- some compound adjectives and nouns where an independent word, for instance *all* or *self*, is used as a prefix:

  all-important

  all-inclusive

  copper-coloured

  half-length

  lean-burn

  old-fashioned

  self-conscious

  self-starter

  user-friendly

- words, particularly words beginning with *re-*, which have two forms with different meanings that would be difficult to distinguish without the hyphen:

  re-cover [the sofa]

  re-creation [of a previously existing organisation]

  re-lease [the building]

Hyphens are often used in:

- nouns made from the basic form of a verb and a preposition:

    link-up

    set-aside

    set-to

    take-off

(These forms are from *The New Oxford Dictionary*; *Bloomsbury* gives *linkup*, but retains hyphens in the other three; *backup* and *setup* are now generally spelt without hyphens. It is, incidentally, incorrect to spell the corresponding verbs as one word or with hyphens, so *to back up, to link up, to set aside* should be used.)

- verbs consisting of a combination of two existing words:

    to ball-watch

    to hang-glide

    to hot-rod

- words in which a confusing or apparently unsayable combination of letters would result if the hyphen were not there:

    bell-like

    de-energise

hip-hop

However, many combinations that would once have been considered confusing, unsayable or just plain unlovely are now widely accepted:

antiaircraft

cooptation

reenter

semiautomatic

Let me just repeat the essential point. The situation with regard to the hyphen is fluid, but fewer and fewer words are being spelt with hyphens. It is not, however, wrong to use a hyphen in, for example, *anti-imperialist* or *co-operative* or *re-engineer*, if you so choose.

Hyphenation before a noun

There are certain combinations of words that are generally spelt without a hyphen when they come after a verb, but with a hyphen when they come before a noun. The best-known examples are probably combinations formed with *well* and *much*:

That fact is well known.

That is a well-known fact.

and

She is well respected in this town.

She is a well-respected citizen of this town.

and

He will be much missed by his colleagues.

We had a surprise visit today from a much-loved and much-missed former colleague.

It is also still a fairly common practice to hyphenate combinations of an adjective and noun or two nouns when they appear in front of another noun:

a floor made of reinforced concrete

a reinforced-concrete floor

support from the grass roots

grass-roots support

Likewise:

a two-year-old child

twenty-four-hour service

a second-class ticket

a two-year contract

However, it is equally common nowadays to find that such hyphens are omitted:

a stainless steel worktop

a three month contract

It is, we might say, only absolutely necessary to insert hyphens where there is a possibility of confusion. For instance, to distinguish between

a large scale model (a scale model that is large; you might even write *a large scale-model*)

and

a large-scale model (a model that is on a large scale)

or to show that

a big-city phenomenon

is one that is characteristic of big cities, not one that is big and occurs in cities.

Hyphens are seldom used in official titles or the names of organisations:

an environmental protection officer

Youth Offending Team

(although, in my opinion, that last phrase ranks as one of the most grotesque examples of politically correct officialese ever created).

There does seem to be one growth area for hyphens, which deserves to be dealt with in this section. People seem to be increasingly inclined to hyphenate combinations of adverbs ending in -*ly* and adjectives in front of nouns. They write about *a gradually-increasing incidence* or *a small but perfectly-formed organ* or *a politically-correct attitude*. Ironically, such combinations are for the most part unnecessary and incorrect. The general rule is that you should hyphenate combinations of adverbs not ending in -*ly* and adjectives:

> *a fast-flowing stream*
>
> *a slow-moving melody*
>
> *a well-kept garden*

but not combinations where the adverb ends in -*ly*:

> *a swiftly flowing stream*
>
> *a slowly declining industry*
>
> *a beautifully kept garden*

except for certain well-established pairings:

> *a fully-fledged chick*
>
> *a highly-strung individual*
>
> *a newly-married couple*

I think it would be possible to argue that *politically(-)correct* should be added to this list, but the dictionaries currently show it as two separate words.

Word-breaking hyphens

Hyphens are used to break words that are too long to fit on to a line. Most word-processing programs will do this for you automatically, if you wish to have it done. If you wish to do this manually, the best advice is to get hold of a spelling dictionary that shows word breaks. The general rules are, however, that the hyphen should be attached to the end of the part of the word that is left on the upper line, not the beginning of the part that is on the lower line; that you should not break words of five letters or fewer; that you should break words between syllables (*time-piece*, NOT *ti-mepiece*) and avoid breaks that could possibly cause confusion (*gen-eral*, NOT *gene-ral*); and that if a word is already hyphenated, you should only break it at the hyphen.

Recap

Hyphens should be used in:

- the written forms of two-word numbers

- words consisting of a combination of more than two other words

- words made by attaching a prefix to a word beginning with a capital letter

- compound adjectives and nouns where an independent word is used as a prefix

- words that have two forms with different meanings that would be difficult to distinguish without the hyphen

- compound adjectives, placed before a noun, containing an adverb that does not end in *-ly*

Hyphens may be used in:

- nouns made from the basic form of a verb and a preposition

- verbs consisting of a combination of two existing words

- compound words with a confusing combination of letters in the middle

- combinations of nouns or nouns and adjectives placed before a noun

Hyphens should not be used:

- to join ordinary two-part words

- to join an adverb ending in -*ly* to an adjective in front of a noun

Exercise

Insert hyphens into the following sentences, where appropriate:

1) *For once, I'd like to spend my holiday in a really high class hotel.*

2) *We don't want any of these Johnny come latelies trying to tell us how to do our jobs.*

3) *I asked the safety inspector for her comments on our new accident prevention policy.*

4) *He's so self effacing that he's almost invisible.*

5) *You won't find a more reasonably priced apartment in such a sought after area of town.*

4 Key to the Exercises

The words or punctuation marks that constitute the correct answers are highlighted in **bold** type.

The Sentence

1) *You **are wanted** urgently back at the office.*

2) *Encouraged by their early success, they **decided** to expand their operations.*

3) *Buying lottery tickets **is** like throwing money down the drain.*

4) *We **shall be going** whatever the weather.*

5) *Whether we like it or not, **we have to follow their instructions**.*

6) *Fortifying himself with a sherry, **he sat down to read the report**.*

7) ***Skip the first paragraph** because I'm going to cut it.*

8) *When you've finished using the sewing machine, **would you mind putting it away?***

The Full Stop

I can't remember exactly when it was that I last saw her. It was a long time ago. I know that because I remember talking to her about what she was going to do when she left school. We were quite close in those days. That changed when she left home and went to university. There she found other friends and forgot about the people back home. It seems to happen like that very often. It's probably my fault for getting old.

The Question Mark

1) *Did you or did you not remove the papers from the folder?*

2) *The question now is where do we go from here.* (This is a statement not a question.)

3) *There were always likely to be difficulties, weren't there?*

4) *I'm not leaving until you tell me whether it's true or not.* (This is an indirect question.)

5) *I wonder if I might ask you a question?*

I really didn't have a clue what he was talking about and wondered whether he had completely lost his mind. Is there such a thing as juvenile dementia? Could it be that he was on drugs? Was it simply that I had completely lost touch with the way that young people think and express themselves? I had never asked myself whether my own ability to communicate might be at fault. The question of whether it might not be began to loom large in my mind.

The Exclamation Mark

1) *What a beautiful day for a picnic!*

2) *Can I help you with anything?*

3) *She never stops talking for a minute!* (or possibly a full stop)

4) *Splash! The little dog leapt into the water to fetch the stick.*

5) *Why didn't you tell me the gun was loaded!* (or possibly a question mark)

6) *Get out of here this minute!*

'The war's over!' People were running out into the streets shouting the good news to their neighbours. What a relief! There would be no more dreading the postman's arrival in case he brought bad news. There would be no more shortages and belt-tightening either. Who could doubt that things were about to get better? There was plenty to recover from, but recovery would be swift, wouldn't it? Of course it would! The war was over. Hurrah!

(alternatively)

Of course it would. The war was over, hurrah!

The Comma

1) *I put on my hat and coat and went out.* (No commas needed.)

2) *The professor, however, had other ideas.*

3) *After you've finished with the book, can I borrow it?*

4) *I sharpened my pencil, adjusted the desk lamp, selected a fresh sheet of paper and prepared to write.*

5) *I've told you before that I don't have any money.* (No commas needed.)

6) *Jean, who was waiting in the wings to go onstage, got a fit of the giggles.*

7) *There isn't really time to do it now, is there?*

8) *When we opened the door, we found ourselves in a warm, cosy, comfortably furnished living room with a bright fire burning in the grate.*

9) *Comrades, I have some bad news for you, I'm afraid.*

10) *We don't, generally, discuss personal matters at committee meetings.*

The woman that I love best in all the world is not, generally speaking, given to acting on impulse. She considers things carefully and then carries out her plans slowly, deliberately and methodically. It takes her a long time to reach a decision, but, once the decision has been made, she sticks to it. As a result, she seldom if ever makes a bad purchase. If she does happen to choose unwisely, however, it takes a very long time to persuade her that she has done so. I, on the other hand, tend to act on the spur of the moment. I am the man for whom returns and refunds were invented, because something that looks irresistible to me in the shop often looks irredeemable when I get it home. Opposites attract, they say. That must be how it is with us, or we should have split up long ago.

The Colon

1) *You made one fatal error: you underestimated your opponent.*

2) *Four players miss this match because of injury: Jones, Lamb, Hall and Myers.*

3) *My life with Matilda Higginbottom: the autobiography of a henpecked husband.*

4) *If I die, I want you to do one thing for me: to make sure that Rover is well looked after.*

The Semicolon

1) *I came; I saw; I conquered.*

2) *Tuesday is when I usually go shopping; Wednesday is when I visit friends.*

3) *They rejected the ultimatum out of hand; thus war became inevitable.*

4) *There are several things you could say: that you are busy that evening; that you can't afford the restaurants they usually go to; that there's a football match that you've promised your sister you'd watch with her; or, quite simply and truthfully, that you don't want to go.*

5) *There was one thing and one thing only that he wanted: true love.*

6) *My brother owns a house in London; my sister rents a flat in Barrow-in-Furness.*

7) *I would help you if I could; it's just that I'm a little busy at the moment.*

8) *It's not the only invitation I've had; in fact, I'm invited out so often I rarely get an evening at home.*

9) *I've had invitations from the following people: Jane, Sara, Jade and, last but not least, Antonia.*

10) *The weather was truly awful for the time of the year: rain followed fog, followed thunder, followed hail.*

Brackets

1) *Benvenuto Cellini (1500–1571) was a famous Italian goldsmith.*

2) *The local speciality is* bouillabaisse *(a kind of fish soup or stew).*

3) *It has been suggested (but not by me) that we should walk the whole way.*

4) *Only three teams (Arsenal, Liverpool and Manchester City) now have any realistic chance of taking the final European place.*

5) *When you arrive (don't be late!), come straight through to the back garden.*

The Dash

1) *I didn't read it all – I simply didn't have enough time – but the bit that I did read was very good.*

2) *They're going to build a new kitchen and conservatory on at the back and landscape the whole garden – if they can find the money, that is.*

3) *The events of the years 1648–1653 had a profound effect on the young king Louis XIV.*

4) *There was no reason – at least, none that Helen was aware of – why they should not be married at once.*

Quotation Marks

1) *Do you spell your name with a 'C' or a 'K'?*

2) *'Let's get out of here,' he whispered.*

3) *You should pronounce the word 'wind' to rhyme with 'kind'.*

4) *'I shall be reciting a very famous poem that begins "If you can keep your head . . .",' he announced.*

5) *She said that it was a very difficult question to answer.* (No quotation marks, as this is indirect speech.)

6) *I know that he calls it a 'dooberry', but what do ordinary people call it?*

7) *She said, 'I'll go and call a cab.'*

8) *'Have you got a pen I could borrow?' he enquired.*

9) *'That', I remarked, 'is something best left for the committee to decide.'* (or *'That,' I remarked . . .*)

10) *He keeps on calling out, 'Where did you put my car keys?'*

11) *'My God!' exclaimed Celia, 'You don't mean he actually asked you to marry him?'*

The Apostrophe

1) *I can't see why he's making so much fuss.*

2) *Those suitcases aren't yours, they're ours.*

3) *That's Peter's book, isn't it?*

4) *The boys' bikes have been left out in the rain.*

5) *It's got its head stuck between the railings.*

6) *I am now going to recite you one of Robert Burns' (or Burns's) most famous poems.*

7) *Where's the Smiths' house?*

8) *Freddy and Jean's aunt gave it to them.*

The Hyphen

1) *For once, I'd like to spend my holiday in a really high-class hotel.*

2) *We don't want any of these Johnny-come-latelies trying to tell us how to do our jobs.*

3) *I asked the safety inspector for her comments on our new accident-prevention policy.*

4) *He's so self-effacing that he's almost invisible.*

5) *You won't find a more reasonably priced apartment in such a sought-after area of town.*

Index

Perfect Babies' Names

Rosalind Fergusson

All you need to choose the ideal name

- Do you want help finding the perfect name?
- Are you unsure whether to go for something traditional or something more unusual?
- Do you want to know a bit more about the names you are considering?

Perfect Babies' Names is an essential resource for all parents-to-be. Taking a close look at over 3,000 names, it not only tells you each name's meaning and history, it also tells you which famous people have shared it over the years and how popular – or unpopular – it is now. With tips on how to make a shortlist and advice for avoiding unfortunate nicknames, *Perfect Babies' Names* is the ultimate one-stop guide.

The *Perfect* series is a range of practical guides that give clear and straightforward advice on everything from getting your first job to choosing your baby's name. Written by experienced authors offering tried-and-tested tips, each book contains all you need to get it right first time.

BOOKS

Perfect Best Man

George Davidson

All you need to know

- Do you want to make sure you're a great best man?
- Do you want to make the groom glad he chose you?
- Do you need some guidance on your role and responsibilities?

Perfect Best Man is an indispensable guide to every aspect of the best man's role. Covering everything from organising the stag night to making sure the big day runs according to plan, it walks you through exactly what you need to do and gives great advice about getting everything done with the least possible fuss. With checklists to make sure you have it all covered, troubleshooting sections for when things go wrong, and a unique chapter on choosing and organising the ushers, *Perfect Best Man* has everything you need to make sure you rise to the occasion.

BOOKS

Perfect CV

Max Eggert

All you need to get it right first time

- Are you determined to succeed in your job search?
- Do you need guidance on how to make a great first impression?
- Do you want to make sure your CV stands out?

Bestselling *Perfect CV* is essential reading for anyone who's applying for jobs. Written by a leading HR professional with years of experience, it explains what recruiters are looking for, gives practical advice about how to show yourself in your best light, and provides real-life examples to help you improve your CV. Whether you're a graduate looking to take the first step on the career ladder, or you're planning an all-important job change, *Perfect CV* will help you stand out from the competition.

BOOKS

Perfect Interview

Max Eggert

All you need to get it right first time

- Are you determined to succeed in your job search?
- Do you want to make sure you have the edge on the other candidates?
- Do you want to find out what interviewers are *really* looking for?

Perfect Interview is an invaluable guide for anyone who's applying for jobs. Written by a leading HR professional with years of experience in the field, it explains how interviews are constructed, gives practical advice about how to show yourself in your best light, and provides real-life examples to help you practise at home. Whether you're a graduate looking to take the first step on the career ladder, or you're planning an all-important job change, *Perfect Interview* will help you stand out from the competition.

BOOKS

Perfect Numerical Test Results

Joanna Moutafi and Ian Newcombe

All you need to get it right first time

- Have you been asked to sit a numerical reasoning test?
- Do you want guidance on the sorts of questions you'll be asked?
- Do you want to make sure you perform to the best of your abilities?

Perfect Numerical Test Results is the ideal guide for anyone who wants to secure their ideal job. Written by a team from Kenexa, one of the UK's leading compilers of psychometric tests, it explains how numerical tests work, gives helpful pointers on how to get ready, and provides professionally constructed sample questions for you to try out at home. It also contains an in-depth section on online testing – the route that more and more recruiters are choosing to take. Whether you're a graduate looking to take the first step on the career ladder, or you're planning an all-important job change, *Perfect Numerical Test Results* has everything you need to make sure you stand out from the competition.

BOOKS

Perfect Personality Profiles

Helen Baron

All you need to make a great impression

- Have you been asked to complete a personality questionnaire?
- Do you need guidance on the sorts of questions you'll be asked?
- Do you want to make sure you show yourself in your best light?

Perfect Personality Profiles is essential reading for anyone who needs to find out more about psychometric profiling. Including everything from helpful pointers on how to get ready to professionally constructed sample questions for you to try out at home, it walks you through every aspect of preparing for a test. Whether you're a graduate looking to take the first step on the career ladder, or you're planning an all-important job change, *Perfect Personality Profiles* has everything you need to make sure you stand out from the competition.

BOOKS

Order more titles in the *Perfect* series
from your local bookshop, or have them delivered
direct to your door by Bookpost.

☐ Perfect Answers to Interview Questions	Max Eggert	9781905211722	£7.99
☐ Perfect Babies' Names	Rosalind Fergusson	9781905211661	£5.99
☐ Perfect CV	Max Eggert	9781905211739	£7.99
☐ Perfect Interview	Max Eggert	9781905211746	£7.99
☐ Perfect Numerical Test Results	Joanna Moutafi and Ian Newcombe	9781905211333	£7.99
☐ Perfect Personality Profiles	Helen Baron	9781905211821	£7.99
☐ Perfect Psychometric Test Results	Joanna Moutafi and Ian Newcombe	9781905211678	£7.99
☐ Perfect Pub Quiz	David Pickering	9781905211692	£6.99
☐ Perfect Readings for Weddings	Jonathan Law	9781905211098	£6.99
☐ Perfect Wedding Speeches and Toasts	George Davidson	9781905211777	£5.99

Free post and packing
Overseas customers allow £2 per paperback

Phone: 01624 677237

Post: Random House Books
c/o Bookpost, PO Box 29, Douglas, Isle of Man IM99 1BQ

Fax: 01624 670 923

email: bookshop@enterprise.net

Cheques (payable to Bookpost) and credit cards accepted

Prices and availability subject to change without notice.
Allow 28 days for delivery.
When placing your order, please state if you do not
wish to receive any additional information.

www.randomhouse.co.uk